Behaviour Assessment Battery

Behaviour Assessment Battery: Assessment of the Cognitive, Communicative and Self-help Skills of the Severely Mentally Handicapped

Behaviour Assessment Battery

Assessment of the Cognitive, Communicative and Self-Help Skills of the Severely Mentally Handicapped

Chris Kiernan, PhD

Thomas Coram Research Unit
University of London Institute of Education
at 41 Brunswick Square
London WC1 1AZ

Malcolm Jones, MSc

Beech Tree Unit
Meldreth near Royston
Herts. SG8 6LG

NFER-NELSON

Published by The NFER-NELSON Publishing Company Ltd.,
Darville House, 2 Oxford Road East,
Windsor, Berks. SL4 1DF
First published by the NFER Publishing Company, 1977
Revised edition by the NFER-NELSON Publishing Company, 1982
© C. Kiernan and M. Jones, 1977, 1982
ISBN 0-7005-0490-7
Code 8132 02 1
1.(4.84)

Typeset by David John Services Ltd., Maidenhead, Berks. SL6 1RR

Printed in Great Britain

Distributed in the USA by Humanities Press Inc.,
Atlantic Highlands, New Jersey 07716 USA.

Contents

ACKNOWLEDGEMENTS

We are grateful to the Department of Health and Social Security, for a grant which allowed us to construct and develop this Battery.

PREFACE TO THE SECOND EDITION

The second edition of *Behaviour Assessment Battery* has allowed some significant revisions. First of all we have been able to add a chapter on the interpretation of the results of the Battery as it relates to the sections themselves and, in particular, to the teaching of communication and self-help skills. Although this does not introduce a hard theoretical element into the Battery it does allow us to provide more suggestions about the significance of results as they bear on programme planning than was the case with the first edition. In addition it allows us to elaborate on the relationship of Battery scores to selection and placement in communication programmes, including those using signs and symbols.

This emphasis on the important developments which have taken place during the last five years in the use of signs and symbols with the mentally handicapped is also reflected in the revision of the Communication Interview and the Expressive and Receptive Vocabulary tests. In each case items relevant to the selection and assessment for signing or symbol use are included, and procedures for assessing responsiveness to speech, sign and symbol outlined. A new procedure, the Sign Imitation Test, was devised specifically to investigate the ability of children or adults to imitate hand postures, positions and movements used in sign languages (Kiernan, Jordan and Saunders, 1978).

The revision has also enabled us to correct a number of errors which were not detected in the first edition. We are grateful to readers for pointing these out to us. We would also like to thank users of the Battery who have taken the trouble to write to us or to talk to us about their experiences with it. The feedback has been very valuable and has helped to shape the revision of the text.

Chris Kiernan
London
March 1981

INTRODUCTION AND RATIONALE

Introduction

The tests in this Battery are designed for use with profoundly handicapped individuals. Testing children or adults in this category is often difficult and requires great skill and also knowledge of the person being tested. Before you use this Battery you should have some experience of testing, although a formal course is not felt to be necessary. The Battery was developed for use by psychologists, doctors, teachers and others who have knowledge and experience with the handicapped. Its purpose is to provide a fuller picture of the person tested than is usually offered by developmental tests.

The current Battery was constructed with the idea in mind that what was important was that the person should achieve certain targets or criterion behaviours in order to function adequately in his environment. The approach can therefore be described as 'criterion-referenced'. This contrasts with most tests of intelligence or development where the reference of the test is to a statistical norm of development derived by examining a group of people at a particular age or ability level. The use of norm-referenced tests with the profoundly handicapped will be discussed in the next section.

Each section of the Battery consists of a set of items and a 'lattice', a visual representation of the sequencing of items. *It is not possible to use the battery adequately by simply scoring the lattice without reference to the text*. Virtually all the value of the battery as a basis for programme planning will be lost if this is done.

The Battery is not intended to replace other methods of assessing the profoundly retarded. Neurological, audiological and visual assessment techniques overlap with several methods and items used in this battery. However, it is necessary for children or adults to be tested by experienced paediatricians, neurologists or audiologists before sound conclusions can be drawn. The approach is intended to be complementary to these other techniques by providing additional or unique detail for the interested educationalist.

Problems of assessment of the profoundly retarded

Assessment of the profoundly retarded presents a wide range of problems. The individuals in this group are frequently multiply-handicapped, showing gross physical problems in addition to mental retardation. Their attentional processes are frequently severely disordered and they are typically uncooperative and difficult to motivate in a test setting. Because of these characteristics there is an almost total absence of suitable assessment instruments developed for use with this group (Shakespeare, 1970). However, with the development of facilities and teaching programmes for the profoundly retarded and with increased provision of services for very young retarded children, it becomes increasingly important to be able to assess suitability of individuals for particular programmes (cf. Mischel, 1968).

The functions of assessment to a large extent dictate the form which assessment must take. Assessment is required at one level to assign individuals to suitable educational facilities. This might be termed administratively-oriented assessment. The emphasis in this type of testing is on need to develop rapid procedures which can provide effective screening. It is typically norm-referenced testing (Glaser, 1963). Despite strong criticism, traditional intelligence testing procedures are clearly of value at this level within existing service patterns (Clarke and Clarke, 1973).

A second type of assessment is needed within any educational setting in order to identify more precise strengths and weaknesses in the abilities of the individual. This type of procedure may be more leisurely than the first since the interest here is in placement in particular programmes rather than in rapid screening. The assessment would therefore be criterion-referenced. It would reflect the curriculum objectives appropriate for the group and may in fact be cast in such terms (e.g. Connor and Talbot, n.d.; Goodfriend, 1972; Jedrysek, Klapper, Pope and Wortis, 1972). The outcome of such an assessment might be in the form of a profile (e.g. Doll, 1953; Frostig, Lefever and Whittlesey, 1964; Gunzburg, 1965; Kirk and McCarthy, 1961) or detailed information in terms of which programmes may be planned (e.g. Bersoff and Greiger, 1971).

Assessment for placement in particular programmes may be termed macro-assessment. It is to be contrasted with assessment related to the modification of particular responses or sets of responses. At this level, a micro-assessment of behaviour in specific contexts in terms of setting, discriminative and reinforcing stimuli may be necessary in order to provide a basis for effective intervention. The particular strength of this type of procedure is that it provides an effective basis for modification of behaviour. However, in more practical contexts, micro-assessment or functional analysis is too time-consuming to be undertaken and is therefore only reasonable when other approaches to modification of behaviour have proved inadequate. In addition, it is often possible to side-step the need for functional analysis by using powerful reinforcers and over-riding the effects of discriminative stimuli controlling existing behaviours (Kiernan, 1973).

Functions of assessment for staff

From the viewpoint of nurses, teachers or care staff, assessment has two clear functions. It can provide guidance on suitable programmes and it can provide a series of goals to be achieved by staff within the framework of these programmes. The extent to which different assessments serve these needs will depend on the type of assessment.

Assessments at the administrative level, normally IQ or other norm reference tests, provide gross directions and goals. Several characteristics of the norm reference test restrict their value in providing guidance on suitable programmes and goals. Firstly, such tests are often constructed in such a way that what are believed to be 'trainable' areas of development are explicitly avoided. To the extent that this goal is achieved, test content *must* be irrelevant to teaching. Secondly, the most effective type of administratively-oriented test will be brief in order to fit the service context in which it is to be used. This very brevity operates against its being of extensive value in specifying teaching programmes. For example, a brief test may indicate that a child has little expressive vocabulary. The brief test is unlikely to be able to go beyond this level of specification of problems because detailed questions concerning sensory, motor, cognitive and environmental factors would be precluded by brevity.

The third and in many ways the most crucial characteristic of norm-referenced tests is that items included in such tests are selected on the basis of their representativeness of particular groups. Items so chosen may or may not be crucial behaviours for development. By 'crucial behaviours' we mean those behaviours without which subsequent development will not occur. Thus block-building is included as a behaviour in most infant tests. Few workers would argue, however, that block-building is in itself a crucial behaviour in development. Rather, the ability to build with blocks provides an index or even merely a correlate of a class of behaviours assumed to be crucial to development because they are related to normal development. Without the significance of behaviours included in norm-referenced tests being spelled out, it is not possible to see how many of them can meaningfully be used to direct teaching.

A fourth argument stems from this point. It is not possible to state conclusively that particular behaviours are crucial in development unless one of two conditions hold. On the one hand, it may be logically necessary that one behaviour occur before another is possible. Thus visual fixation logically precedes visual tracking, production of words logically precedes production of meaningful sentences, the ability to bear weight on the legs logically precedes walking.

The second possibility is that it can be demonstrated that behaviour B *never* occurs before behaviour A. In this case, two behaviours which may be theoretically linked but which do not logically imply one another are shown to be related. This relation may result from a correlation of either A or B with other factors. For example, the occurrence of behaviour C. And it may be the occurrence of C rather than A which is a necessary and sufficient condition for occurrence of B. If we know only about normal developmental sequences, we may incorrectly assume that A 'caused' B. In order to detect the C-B relation as opposed to the A-B relation, we would have to be able to independently manipulate A and C.

In other words, it is not possible to say that particular behaviours are crucial to normal development unless an experimental teaching approach is used. It is only through experimental manipulation of possible sequences of teaching skills that clear information on the viability of alternate approaches can be obtained. What can be stated quite categorically is that the item listing in norm-referenced tests does not necessarily indicate such sequences.

A fifth argument concerning the use of norm-referenced tests to guide nurses, teachers or parents in teaching children again arises from the selection constraints operating in these tests. Items are eliminated to give a short list of reliable items. However, an item may be reliable without being 'crucial' in development. Reliability will depend partly on the behaviour concerned and partly on the skill of the test constructor in devising items. Therefore, it is quite possible that crucial behaviours will be excluded because test procedures for assessing these items are not as reliable as for less crucial items.

In the hypothetical example shown on the next page only one item from the 'crucial' sequence shows higher reliability than the 'non-crucial correlate'. Therefore, if these items were being selected for reliability in a test, the items underlined would be selected.

Crucial Sequence	Reliability	Non-Crucial Correlates	Reliability
A	0.65	A[1]	0.76
B	0.91	B[1]	0.21
C	0.48	C[1]	0.71
D	0.64	D[1]	0.94

Similarly one or two steps in a sequence crucial to development may be poorly sampled or items may be of low reliability. So far as the final test outcome is concerned, this will lead to a patchiness in coverage, with conceivably more coverage of less important items. In our hypothetical example only one item from the crucial sequence would appear.

These arguments all suggest that administratively-oriented norm-referenced tests are fundamentally unsuitable for use in guidance of teaching. This is not to deny their clear value in the general administrative context or in indicating gross developmental changes in research contexts. All that is being claimed is that they are unsuitable for guiding teaching.

On the other hand, macro- or micro-assessment procedures are geared to indicating suitability of individuals for particular programmes and specifying goals for staff. Such assessment procedures may contain a further advantage for staff dealing with the profoundly retarded by allowing structure and feedback to be given where goals are often difficult to set and progress slow (Kiernan, 1973; Panyan, Boozer and Morris, 1970). Structure and feedback can best be provided by criterion-referenced assessments which allow close integration of assessment and teaching.

Such assessments can be developed at either macro- or micro-assessment levels. We have already suggested that micro-assessment procedures are often impractical and may not be necessary in many cases, provided other conditions can be met. Therefore it seems of value to explore macro-assessment procedures as a means to providing further guidance to teachers and others involved in modification of the behaviour of the profoundly retarded.

A survey of current macro-assessment procedures reveals substantial problems. Of the few possible procedures, the majority fail to provide a sufficiently low floor, having been devised for normal children of pre-school age or moderately retarded individuals. Most do not allow for motivational problems and failure to comprehend instructions (Shakespeare, 1970). A final problem is the failure to provide a logical developmental sequencing of steps on which to base teaching. In other words their sequencing is often as illogical as that seen in norm-referenced tests.

The Behaviour Assessment Battery
Objectives

The Behaviour Assessment Battery (BAB) was devised in an attempt to provide a basis for macro-assessment which would achieve the following objectives:

(a) To give a broad coverage of behaviour, including self-help skills, cognitive and emotional aspects of behaviour, in order to allow a comprehensive programme to be devised;

(b) To provide a standardized testing procedure within a framework which was flexible in terms of motivation of the individuals in the test situation and in the testing procedures used. The procedure involves an attempt to isolate rewards to be used in the test setting and flexible specification of some test settings to allow greater freedom in item testing;

(c) To provide a battery which would coordinate with existing procedures and macro-assessment batteries by extending their coverage downwards to cover the profoundly handicapped. No attempt has been made to replace existing procedures, simply to develop items and procedures to fill the gaps left by test floors which are too high to sample the behaviour of the profoundly handicapped, or to substitute for procedures which are not appropriate for the profoundly retarded because of their reliance on understanding of language or responsiveness to social reinforcement.

In line with the objectives of the Battery, items to be used in formal or semi-formal settings had to meet certain criteria. Firstly they had to be written or re-written in order to cut out the influence of the child's understanding of instructions as far as was predictable. In many cases instructions like 'keep watching the object' become less critical if the examiner can use an object which is very interesting to the child. The selection and use of such objects is essential for the successful use of the BAB.

Other items can be demonstrated to the child or he can be prompted by pointing or by physical guidance. Under these circumstances the examiner records whether demonstration (D), prompting by pointing (P) or physical guidance (PG) has been necessary in relation to any item.

In other cases the child is pre-trained to allow him to learn how to 'play the game'. The Communication Section contains four components of this type, concerned with Motor and Verbal Imitation and Expressive and Receptive Vocabulary. These components follow a procedure developed by Diane and Bill Bricker in which the child is pre-tested and if necessary pre-trained on very simple examples of the test items. For example the Verbal Imitation component is pre-tested by the child being asked to imitate 'a' (as in father) and 'mmm'. The objectives of pre-training are to get the child to attend, and to produce the correct response at the appropriate time at an audible level. If the child needs pre-training then the correct responses are rewarded using incentives known to be effective with the individual. Given pre-training, the child has a better chance of being able to demonstrate his abilities.

In the case of all items and sections it is essential that the child attend to the examiner on request. We have found it valuable on occasions to pre-train the child for twenty or so trials by prompting and rewarding the child to look at examiner on the request 'Look . . . '. In addition a pre-training phase in which the child is rewarded for sitting in quiet activity rather than running round the test room may avoid the disruptive effects of so-called hyperactive behaviour. A ten or twenty minute pre-training period may again be an excellent investment.

A major shift in emphasis from normal to BAB testing procedures lies in the explicit use of adequate incentives for correct responding on test items. The majority of test procedures assume that the child will be adequately motivated either by the reward of task completion or by the minimal social reward allowed in the testing situation. Such subtle rewards are often inadequate for the mentally handicapped who consequently may score well below their actual abilities if standardized testing conditions are maintained. The BAB standardization was conducted with the in-built assumption that adequate incentives are identified either by observation or interview with parents, nurses or teachers before the Battery is used. These incentives are then used either as objects in test items or as rewards for correct performance. For example, if it is known that the child is particularly fond of one toy, dislikes physical contact but enjoys an adult singing a pop song and also likes fizzy drinks then the toy can be used to examine fixation, tracking or object permanence, and appropriate performance can be reinforced by the examiner singing and by occasional fizzy drinks.

Those who know the very severely handicapped will recognize that their preferences and dislikes are often highly idiosyncratic. As with all testing situations even a child who is highly capable will do nothing unless adequately motivated. It is essential that good incentives are isolated and used appropriately to elicit and reward behaviour if the very severely handicapped are to be fairly tested.

In our experience it is usually possible to identify at least a few adequate incentives for each individual by interviewing parents, nurses and teachers. These may then be used in conjunction with preferences which emerge in the testing situation to motivate and reward the child.

One consequence of the approach is that the equipment used in many sections can not be standardized for all individuals. Since the purpose of the Battery is to see how the child performs given optimal conditions, the precision offered by standardized equipment has to be sacrificed if strong preferences appear. Nonetheless considerable standardization of equipment has been possible. Details of equipment are given in a later section.

Assumptions about the assessment environment

As can be seen from this discussion the BAB assumes that the examiner will be willing to expend a fair amount of time on administering the Battery. The full Battery may require the examiner to spend up to six or seven twenty-minute sessions with the child, plus an interview with parents and teachers lasting an hour each. However there is nothing to prevent the examiner from using only one or two sections in isolation and although the dual interview may reveal valuable information on discrepancies between school and home behaviour parent interviews may themselves be enough if thoroughly discussed in programme development discussions.

Assumptions about the teaching environment

The BAB is explicitly teaching or training oriented. In other words, it is assumed that the purpose of the assessment on the Battery is to set up training programmes. Given this assumption, others concerning the teaching environment must follow. It is assumed that the teaching setting provides a good supply of educational materials and a good motivational setting. From a motivational viewpoint, the Battery assumes a social environment with the possibility of one-to-one and small group teaching and a willingness to use social, sensory or material reinforcers contingently on appropriate performance.

Development of the Behaviour Assessment Battery
There were three phases in the development of the Behaviour
Assessment Battery.

(1) *Construction of item bank*
Phase One involved surveying existing test and interview batteries
for the mentally handicapped or their guardians and for the infant
or pre-school child. Seventy-one such instruments were examined.
Additional items were gleaned from the experimental and theoretical
literature, in particular from discussions of normal infant development (e.g. Cratty, 1970; Piaget, 1952). Finally, items were developed
during testing as need or suggestion indicated.

(2) *Construction of the Battery*
Items were divided into those optimally valuable in the formal or
semi-formal setting, items optimally suitable for observation and
items which were best suited for interview coverage. Items in the first
two categories, the Test Battery Behavioural Items were rearranged
into sections, e.g. inspection, search strategies. Interview items were
similarly arranged. In some cases sections involve both interview and
behavioural items.

(3) *Administration during development*
During its development the following samples of subjects were used:
    (a) Queen Mary's Hospital for Children, Carshalton. Thirty-
six children were given the behavioural items including test-
retests. An earlier version of the interview was used for 40 children
on a test-retest basis. A further 28 children were given the imitation
assessments only. Age range of children: 6 years 3 months to
17 years 1 month.
    (b) Camden Road Nursery for Preschool Mentally Handi-
capped Children, 404 Camden Road, London N7. Eighteen
children were given the behavioural items. The interview schedule
was completed for 17 children. The age range was 2 years 2 months
to 5 years 6 months.
    (c) Hornsey Centre for Handicapped Children, Muswell Hill,
London N10. Fifty children were tested and retested on the
behavioural items. Twenty-two children were tested once on
earlier versions. The age range was 2 years 3 months to 6 years
4 months.

(d) Harperbury Hospital, Harper Lane, St Albans. Twenty children were tested and 15 retested on behavioural items. The age range was 7 years 8 months to 16 years 4 months.

(e) Meldreth Manor School, Royston, Herts. Seventeen children were tested on the behavioural items. The age range was 9 years 11 months to 15 years 5 months.

In all, 174 children were tested in the development of the behavioural items. One hundred and eleven children were used in the development of the interview schedule. The difference in number of children used reflects greater difficulty in development of the behavioural items. Seventy-six individuals were assessed in early versions of the behavioural item set. One hundred and three were assessed on the final battery. A further 80 children were tested on the final version of the imitation schedules, and 54 on vocabulary sections. Seventy-one individuals were assessed on the final version of the interview schedule. These data are summarized in Table 3 (page 25).

	Behavioural Items			*Interview Schedule*	
	Early Versions	Final Versions			
			Test-		
		Single	Retest	Early	Final
QMH	36	-	-	40	-
Camden Road	18	-	-	-	17
Hornsey Centre	22	30	36	-	54
Harperbury	-	5	15	-	-
Meldreth	-	17	-	-	-
Totals	76	52	51	40	71

All individuals were classified as severely or profoundly retarded by relevant authorities.

Elimination of items
Items were eliminated if they did not achieve certain criteria.

(a) *Specificity of statement.* Very general items were excluded or modified by rendering them more specific.

(b) *Reliance on test instructions.* Items in which test instructions could not be reframed to allow gestural indication or administration without verbal test instructions were eliminated, or alternatively classified as relating to receptive vocabulary.

(c) *Items involving distress* to the testee were not included.

(d) *Items on which all individuals scored or on which none of the sample scored* were eliminated.

(e) *Items with low inter-observer agreement were modified and eliminated* if modification did not improve agreement beyond 90 %.

(f) *Test-Retests Reliabilities.* Items were not normally excluded on the basis of low test-retest reliability. Reliabilities were calculated on the basis of sections. These coefficients are included below.

Final structure of the Behaviour Assessment Battery
(I) *Types of item*
The final battery consists of two types of item:

(a) *Interview schedule items* The schedule is administered to the nurse, teacher, parent or other guardian of the individual. The items are used as a basis for discussion. The interview should be tape recorded and coded after administration.

(b) *Behavioural items*
(i) *Observational items* A small group of items are covered in the assessment by observation of the child's general behaviour.

(ii) *Test items* These items form the bulk of the Behavioural Items and relate to semi-formal test sessions. Test items were administered either in a quiet, distraction-free test room or in a Mobile Laboratory. The bulk of items were administered either on the floor or at a table.

(iii) *Pre-training — test components* As already mentioned above in the assessment of motor and verbal imitation and receptive and expressive vocabulary, it was found that individuals tested were often unable to follow test instructions. However, collateral evidence from parents or nurses suggested that they could demonstrate the abilities examined, given appropriate motivation and understanding of test requirements. The pre-training — test procedures were therefore adopted.

Pre-training consisted of up to 40 training trials on a simplified version of the test behaviour. For example, for motor imitation, two simple behaviours are trained over the 40 trial period. During this phase, the individual is prompted and rewarded as necessary. The aim of the pre-training phase in this and other cases is to teach the individual tested the requirements of the test setting; to teach him how to 'play the game'. However, data showing learning or failure to learn during pre-training may in itself be of value in indicating the level of required teaching.

Test Phase. A number of different tasks are presented and usually represented in order to examine behaviour in a more controlled setting than the pre-training setting.

(2) *Coverage of the Battery*
The Battery covers the following areas:

General information
1. (R) Reinforcement and Experience (Interview).
2. (I) Inspection (Test).
3. (T) Tracking (Test).
4. (V) Visuo-Motor (Test).
5. (A) Auditory (Test plus Interview).
6. (PC) Postural Control (Interview).
7. (E) Exploratory Play (Test).
8. (CP) Constructive Play (Test).
9. (SS) Search Strategies (Test).
10. (P) Perceptual Problem Solving (Test).
11. (So) Social (Test plus Interview).
12. (C) Communication (Training, Test and Interview).
13. (SH) Self-Help Skills (Interview).

The interview sections may be administered in any order. For a child who is not known to the examiner Sections 6, Postural Control and 12, Self-Help Skills, provide a useful initial basis of knowledge about the child. The examiner should be prepared to re-organize the interview to catch useful leads. This remark applies particularly to problem behaviours. It is easier to deal with discussion of problem behaviours when they arise in the natural flow of a discussion rather than waiting until they arise in the directed course of the interview. For this reason Section 1 on Reinforcement and Experience which deals with a range of problem behaviours may best be left to the end of the interview.

Sections of the BAB may be administered in the order indicated or in other orders. It is however necessary to identify adequate rewards before attempting later sections. Administration of the interview

before test items can also provide a useful background in relation to
postural control and problem behaviours which can make test administration more efficient.

(3) *Equipment*
  The equipment for the BAB is listed in Table 1 with the exception
of equipment for Section 11 — Communication — which is listed in
Table 2. Equipment which can be used in common in Section 11
and the rest of the BAB is indicated in Table 2.

(4) *Scoring*
  Each section comprises a series of items which can be summarized
on a scoring lattice. Each lattice consists of a series of
related items arranged vertically on stems. Each stem may have up
to ten items. In general a stem represents a particular type of task,
function or setting which can relate to a particular set of teaching
situations. The lattice may consist of up to six stems.
  Within each lattice items are scaled in such a way that the easier
items are at the base of the lattice with progressively more difficult
items toward the top of the lattice. Difficulty is assessed by frequency
of occurrence in the sample of children. The more frequently occurring
items were assumed to be the easiest, the least frequent the most
difficult or advanced.
  Items in sections are numbered within and across stems of the
lattice. The left hand stem is numbered first, then the second from left
and so on. Items are identified by a section code (V — Visuo Motor;
SS — Search Strategies; I — Inspection etc., see page 19, and so on)
item number indicating its position in the section lattice.
  Where items occur in more than one section a cross-reference to
the other section is given by putting the cross-referenced item number
in brackets following the item. So I13 (So2) means that item Inspection
13 is the same as item Social 2. From the viewpoint of administration
and scoring of the Battery there is clearly no need to repeat items of
this type. There are 125 items in all in the sections. Of these, 32 are
repeat items.
  There are 15 lattices. Reinforcement and Experience is not summarized on a lattice. Each other section has one lattice with the exception of Communication which is broken down into lattices on
Understanding, Imitation and Expression with an overall programme
lattice also included.

Table 1: Equipment for BAB Sections 1–10 and 13

SECTIONS

	I	T			E	CP	SS	P	
Small torch	/	/							
10, 2 cms red cubes in box	/		/					/	
6, 12 cms toys, 3 squeaky toys, 1 white object	/	/	/	/	/		/	/	/
3 toy cars	/	/	/		/		/	/	/
Picture book	/								/
Selection of sweets including red sweets c 1·5 cms diameter	/						/	/	
10 sheets A4 paper plain	/					/			
Nylon or felt tipped pens or crayons	/					/			
Colour discs	/								
Silent pull-along toy		/	/		/				
Ball (about 5 cms diameter)		/	/		/	/			/
2, 20 cms × 30 cms opaque screens		/					/	/	
1 transparent screen, 20 cms × 20 cms								/	
Soft pad		/					/		
Stand, 40 cms × 40 cms × 6 cms			/						
Chime bars				/	/				
Small hand bell				/	/				
Rattle				/	/				
Large plastic nut and bolt					/				
Screw barrels					/				
Spectacle case					/				

Table 1 (continued)

SECTIONS

	I	T	V	A	E	CP	SS	P	So
6, 1 cm × 5 cms dowels in peg board					/				
Tambourine					/				
10, 4, 5 cms wooden cubes				/	/	/			
Tin foil					/				
Newspaper					/				
2, sandpaper boards, 12 cms × 12 cms					/				
Ring or toy attached to 60 cms string					/				
Waste paper basket						/			
Stacking toy with blind ring						/			
3, half ball covers							/	/	
Orange cloth 300 cms × 300 cms							/	/	
3 small boxes, e.g. 10 cms × 10 cms, with easily opened lids.						/			
Cord, 600 cms								/	
Toy rake								/	
Suction cup with perspex platform								/	
Rattling stick								/	
String of beads								/	
Narrow necked container								/	
Mirror									/
Search and Perceptual Problem Solving Apparatus							/	/	

Table 2: Equipment for BAB Section 11: Communication.

Motor Imitation Pre-training (Pages 131 to 132). Two squeaky toys, two cups, two wooden beads.

Motor Imitation Test (pages 132 to 134). Two cups; two small bells; four 4.5 cm square blocks; two balls; two sets two graduated cups; two hats; two spoons; two toy cars; two tambourines; two drumsticks; two pull along cars; two bracelets; two combs; one sheet A4 paper; two crayons, felt or nylon tipped pens; two whistles; two boxes 10 cms square. (The squeaky toys, blocks, cars, paper, pens and boxes are available from the other sections of the BAB as is one cup, one bell, one ball and one car.)

Verbal Imitation Pretest and Test (pages 134 to 135). Tape recorder.

Sign Imitation Test (pages 135 to 140). No equipment required.

Expressive Vocabulary Pretest (pages 122 to 123). Tape recorder; bottle, flower.

Expressive Vocabulary Test (pages 122 to 127). Tape recorder. List 1, wooden block, toy lorry, toy car, ball, baby doll, toy hammer, cup, hat, watch, toy train, clock, toy boat, toy saucepan, toy cat, apple; List 2, toy bus, spoon, toy chair, hairbrush, book, toy telephone, plate, toy table, box, shoe, glass, sock, toy fish, nail, toy bird.

Receptive Vocabulary Pretest (pages 127 to 128). Hat, baby doll.

Receptive Vocabulary Test (pages 128 to 130). List 1. Cup, clock, plate, spoon, watch, scissors, apple, ball, toy car, pencil; List 2. Shoe, toy chair, book, glass, sock, toy telephone, toy table, knife, hat, box.

Items should be scored directly on to the lattices. We have found it useful to xerox score sheets and then to strike the items through with red felt pen when the child has achieved criterion on that item: If the child has needed a demonstration this is indicated by a (D) next to the item. Prompting by pointing (P) and physical guidance (PG) preceding correct performance can also be indicated on the lattice. Failed items are indicated — on the relevant lattice item.

Analysis of Behaviour Assessment Battery

Test-retest reliabilities were computed for each section with three months between test administrations. In addition, per cent agreement between observers was computed where relevant. Guttman coefficients of reproducibility were calculated for eleven sections, along with minimal marginal reproducibility (Edwards, 1957; Goodenough, 1944). These statistics are included in Table 3 (see page 25).

The Guttman statistic reflects the degree to which the items in the section scale in such a way that any given total score reflects a unique order of scoring. Thus on a four point scale with items A, B, C and D a score of two would reflect correct responses on say responses A and B but not on C and D. In the items on a Guttman scale one would expect all subjects scoring two to score on items A and B rather than any other two items out of four. Subjects scoring three score on items A, B and C but not D. Similarly a score of one would always represent a score on one particular item namely A. In other terms given any total score the items passed and failed are precisely predictable if the scale is a pure Guttman scale.

Guttman analysis is felt to be appropriate with the current battery since we are looking at scales which are intended for use in guidance of teaching. Therefore one would hope that items would scale in such a way as to suggest a progression from simpler to more complex tasks. All other factors being equal, the closer the coefficient of reproducibility approaches 1.00, the closer the scale approaches a perfect progression.

Unfortunately the coefficient of reproducibility is affected by the overall distribution of scores in the sample of individuals. If many subjects score highly on items in the section then the coefficient will be inflated by this alone (cf. Edwards, 1957). The extent to which the coefficient of reproducibility is affected is assessed by a statistic termed minimal marginal reproducibility. A comparison of minimal marginal reproducibility and the coefficient of reproducibility gives an indication of the extent to which scaling affects scores. High coefficients of reproducibility coupled with low minimal marginal reproducibility statistics indicate that behaviours scale in such a way that the 'developmental sequences' involved are fairly clear cut and invariant as reflected in the sample concerned.

Table 3: Summary Statistics of the BAB

	Section	Co-eff. of Reproducibility	mmr	t-rt r	% agreement
1.(R)	Reinforcement and Experience				
2.(I)	Inspection	0.89	0.61	0.95	83.96
3.(T)	Tracking	0.93	0.65	0.82	85.56
4.(V)	Visuo-Motor	0.91	0.74	0.87	85.24
5.(A)	Auditory	0.78	0.54	0.68	72.00
6.(PC)	Postural Control	-	-	-	0.99*
7.(E)	Exploratory Play	0.76	0.46	0.90	81.19
8.(CP)	Constructive Play	0.95	0.47	0.82	92.38
9.(SS)	Search Strategies	0.91	0.63	0.96	88.70
10.(P)	Perceptual Problem Solving	0.86	0.68	0.94	92.86
11.(So)	Social	0.81	0.56	0.67	79.64
12.(C)	Communication				
13.(SH)	Self-Help Skills	-	-	+	-

* Inter-observer reliability
+ Inter-interviewer reliability components:
  Feeding 0.98, Dressing 0.95, Washing 0.90, Toileting 0.96

1981 Revisions and additions to the 1977 Battery

The second edition of *Behaviour Assessment Battery* has been modified to include a revised and updated interview on communication, revised procedures for assessing receptive and expressive vocabulary, and a test of ability to imitate hand shapes for children who are either in a sign language programme or are being considered for sign language teaching.

The Communication Interview. The revision of the Communication Interview was felt to be desirable given the substantial growth in the use of sign languages and symbol systems in the late 1970s (Jones, Reid and Kiernan, 1982; Kiernan, Reid and Jones, 1982). The revised interview represents in part a reorganization of the 1977 version. Additional items, derived from work on communication which is currently under way (Kiernan, 1981a) have been included in order to broaden the coverage and render the interview more directly relevant to work with children without speech who may be in a sign and symbol programme. The original reliabilities on the interviews do not hold for the revised versions and no re-standardization has been attempted. However, the additional items have been drawn from procedures which have been extensively developed and for which reliabilities are high (Kiernan, 1981a).

Sign Imitation Test. The test of ability to imitate hand shapes was developed in 1977 as the Imitation Test but it will be referred to here as the Sign Imitation Test (Kiernan and Reid, 1977). The test was devised as a method of gathering information on the ability of young and mentally handicapped subjects to imitate hand postures and palm directions. The test may be used either as a means of selection for sign language programmes or during such programmes as a means of assessing the progress of students in acquiring frequently-used hand postures, orientations and movements. Other measures of ability to imitate hand postures are mainly related to neurological assessment and involve restricted ranges of postures (Berges and Lezire, 1965; Rutter, Graham and Yule, 1970). The Sign Imitation Test differs from the Motor Imitation Test included in the BAB in relating specifically to the movements and hand postures used in sign languages and systems. The Motor Imitation Test assesses the ability to imitate responses concerned with objects and with gross body movement.

The Sign Imitation Test comprises five sub-sections. The first assesses hand preference; the next two, the ability to imitate hand postures; the fourth, ability to imitate palm directions and the fifth, ability to imitate the hand and arm movements used in sign languages. Hand postures included in the test were selected by analysing the signs for 39 commonly used words (Stage One, Makaton Vocabulary, Walker, 1976). Each word was 'translated' into British Sign Language (Jones, 1972; Sutcliffe, 1972), American Sign Language (Stokoe, Casterline and Croneberg, 1965; Riekehof, 1963) and the Paget Gorman Sign System (Paget, Gorman and Paget, 1972). Where a sign involved two hands, each adopting a different posture, both hands were scored. Similarly where one hand adopted two postures within a sign both were scored.

The ten commonest postures were chosen for inclusion in the Sign Imitation Test. Of these postures Flat Hands accounted for 23.2 per cent of all postures used, Fist Hands 14.7 per cent, Scoop Hands 9.6 per cent and Index Hands 8.5 per cent. Other postures accounted for smaller proportions of the total. The Paget L Hand was used by the Paget system but not in the British Sign Language sample.

The Y Hand and the Crossed Second, Third, Fourth Finger Hand (C2, 3, 4fh) were added in order to represent more complex postures. The Y hand was used by Berges and Lezire (1965) and shown to produce problems for normal children up to the age of six. The C2, 3, 4fh is among those acquired late in development by young deaf children (McIntyre, 1974). These postures extend the potential scope of the test.

Palm directions and movements were selected rationally from a consideration of those used in the sign languages and systems.

Analysis of the Sign Imitation Test. The first four sections of the test were administered to 36 children between the ages of 4 years 8 months and 13 years 4 months at two schools for severely educationally subnormal children, Queen Elizabeth II Jubilee School and William C. Harvey School. Fifteen of the children were girls, 21 were boys. The test was administered a second time after a four- to five-month gap to 20 of the children in order to assess test-retest reliability.

Hand preference. Section One of the test comprises five items designed to establish hand preference. The hand preferred on this section is the one for which signs were modelled, where relevant, in subsequent sections.

Thirty-three children provided usable data. Of these children 24 showed at least four responses with the right or left hand. The remainder showed a three to two majority preference. Of the 24 children in the first group 20 were right handed (83.3 per cent); in the second group six of the nine children showed more right than left responses. There were no differences between boys and girls in hand preference.

Twenty children were retested after three months by a different tester. Of these children 15 showed right hand preference on the first test, five left. On retest seven children showed a change in preference. Five children shifted from right to left, two from left to right. In three cases the shift was dramatic, four or five responses being to one side on the test and to the other on retest.

These data would be of concern if the hand preference test were to be seen as critical to the validity of later components of the Sign Imitation Test. However, it was included here only to eliminate possible biassing in the test procedure. Consequently instability of preference is allowed for by its inclusion.

Hand postures.   In this section children were shown the 12 hand postures modelled by the tester with one hand and asked to imitate them.

The 36 children ranged in their scores from three to 12 items correct. Three postures, Fist Hand (35), Flat Hand (34) and Index Hand (34) were the most commonly correct. The Scoop Hand (26), O Hand (22) and Compressed Hand (19) were imitated correctly by over 50 per cent of children followed by C2, 3 4f Hand (16), 1, 2f Hand (15), Y Hand (14) and V Hand (13). The Right Angle Index Hand (11) and Paget L Hand (8) proved most difficult.

The data showed that the earliest responses to appear in normal development — Flat, Fist and Index Hand responses — are the easiest to imitate. Responses requiring independent action of the second and third fingers which are linked by intertendinous connections were more difficult to imitate, again reflecting sequences in normal development (Hollinshead, 1960).

One finding which is of interest is that postures which are used more frequently in the sample of signs drawn are also easier to imitate. The correlation between the frequency of usage overall and ease of imitation is +0.73 (df=11, p < 0.01). This finding suggests that sign languages have 'selected' easier postures for more frequent use. Interestingly, the lowest correlation between ease of imitation and use by a system is between ease and frequency of use in the Paget Gorman Sign System (r = 0.50, df = 11, p < 0.05).

Scalogram analysis of the items produced a RepA value of 0.793. With RepI at 0.238 this gives an Index of Consistency (I) of 0.728 (Green, 1956). Since it is suggested that I values of more than 0.5 indicate scalability this suggests a satisfactory scaling of items. This would imply that if a child or adult can score at all he will be likely to imitate the Flat, Fist and Index Hands. Since these represent very common postures in sign languages and systems even this relatively low score may be an indicator of value of sign teaching. We will take up this theme in the next chapter.

Analysis of the pattern of errors on the Sign Imitation Test allows some inferences to be drawn concerning sensible remedial steps. The patterns of error observed will be described more fully in the next chapter.

Twenty children were re-tested on this section four to five months after initial testing. The resulting correlation of test and retest scores is +0.707 (df=19, p <0.01).

Combinations. In the combination condition subjects are asked to imitate ten two-handed signs with a different posture being adopted by each hand in six of the ten signs. Thirty-six children completed the original testing. The order of frequency of correct postures was equivalent to that for the one-hand condition. There were no differences apparent between ease of imitation of right and left hand postures given equivalent difficulty of posture.

The order of difficulty of combinations is given in the Test itself. Scalogram analysis, computed on frequency of both hands, gave a RepA of 0.814. Since RepI was 0.236 the Index of Consistency was 0.756, again suggesting scalability. The pattern of errors in combinations will be discussed in the next chapter.

Palm direction. In this section subjects are asked to imitate orientations of the hand which direct the palm in directions used by languages and systems. This section produced the fewest errors. Of the 34 children completing the first test 20 scored five out of five, seven scored four out of five and seven three out of five. Thirteen of the 20 children who completed the retest scored five, five scored four and only two scored three.

The test-retest correlation was low (r=+0.06, df=19, p > 0.05), probably because of the tight distribution of scores.

Movement. The movement section was added after the initial development of the test, and no systematic data has been collected on this section. It is included here in the interest of completeness.

Expressive and receptive vocabulary. The original expressive and receptive vocabulary procedures have been retained with only minor amendments. Additional procedures have been suggested for children in sign or symbol programmes.

The typical sign language or symbol system programme combines the use of speech and augmentative cues (Kiernan, Reid and Jones, 1982). It is usually suggested that teachers or therapists speak as they sign or indicate symbols. There are variants of this 'Total Communication' approach. Advocates of some systems suggest that key words should be signed and a whole sentence spoken (Walker, 1978). Advocates of other systems suggest that all words spoken should be matched by signs (Craig, 1978). Although there is no evidence to suggest that one approach is superior to another (Reid and Kiernan, 1982) there are common reports of improvements in the understanding and use of speech within signing and symbol programmes (Kiernan, Reid and Jones, 1982). However there are big individual differences in development, and evidence provided by Carr and others suggests the need to assess the extent to which the child is responding to different aspects of the sign-speech or symbol-speech complex (Carr, Binkoff, Kologinsky and Eddy, 1978). Carr and his colleagues tested children who had been taught to sign using a Total Communication procedure. They were interested to see which aspect of the presentation procedure — the spoken word, lip movements or the appearance of the object — the child was using as a cue to sign. They used a procedure in which each aspect of the complex was tested separately (derived from work of Lovaas and Schriebman, 1971). So, for the spoken word condition, they said the word whilst covering the mouth, so that the child could not lip read; the lip-reading condition involved mouthing the word silently; and the object condition involved the simple presentation of the object without speech. They found that one child responded to both the spoken word and the sign. The other three children responded only to the sight of the object. None of the children responded to the lip-reading condition.

Other authors have used a parallel procedure to assess receptive vocabulary (e.g. Baron and Isensee, 1976; Carr and Dores, 1981; Webster, McPherson, Sloman, Evans and Kuchar, 1973). Speech alone or sign alone was presented in probe trials following Total Communication teaching using both speech and sign. Two of Carr and Dores's subjects, neither of whom had any speech or significant speech sounds, responded only to the signs. The other four children in the study, all of whom had good verbal imitation skills, responded to *both* word and sign (Carr, 1979). This result suggests that an initial level of vocal imitative ability is necessary before the child can respond to the verbal element of a Total Communication procedure.

The procedures described in these studies have been adapted for use with symbols in addition to signs, and are included in the revision of the BAB tests for Expressive and Receptive Vocabulary.

Final comment

In this chapter we have described the reasons for the development of the BAB, the methods used in development and the structure and statistical analyses of the Battery. Since the Battery was first published in 1977 the need for such an instrument has probably increased rather than diminished with the increasing tendency to develop the structured programmes which the Battery presumes (Kiernan and Jones, 1980). In the current edition we have also extended the coverage of the Battery in order to provide a framework for the assessment of children for and within sign and symbol teaching programmes.

THE USE AND INTERPRETATION OF THE BEHAVIOUR ASSESSMENT BATTERY

In this chapter we will set out some suggestions for how the BAB may most valuably be used and how data from it may be interpreted for the development of programmes.

As we pointed out in the last chapter the procedures described were standardized in work with severely handicapped children and young people. As such, they represent a rare and possibly still unique collection of data. There are, of course, many checklists which have been devised through work with the mentally handicapped. The authors of some of these have presented data on their reliability (e.g. Gunzburg, 1973), but in the case of many others the checklists are essentially *ad hoc*. Several test procedures have also been developed which overlap with the BAB in coverage. These have, typically, been developed with non-handicapped populations. The most notable procedures of this type are the Uzgiris-Hunt Scales (Uzgiris and Hunt, 1975). These scales were developed from Piagetian thinking which also formed the basis for the initial development of the BAB scales (Jones, 1971). We will make some comparisons of relevant sections of the BAB and Uzgiris-Hunt scales as we progress through this chapter.

As we pointed out in the last chapter the BAB sections are designed to complement other test procedures which may be being used with the handicapped individual. This they can do because they employ a larger number of items than many other procedures and can therefore serve to fill out pictures sketched in by other procedures. They also cover more fundamental levels of development than most other tests. In other words they can cover behaviour which is below the test 'floor' of many procedures. Some areas, for example the development of visual discrimination, are not covered because we found that item sequences from other test procedures covered the levels we wished to explore (e.g. Bayley, 1969). Visual discrimination skills are also covered in a slightly different format by Kiernan (1981b).

The BAB can be used in several different ways. On the one hand it can be used, along with other procedures, as part of a systematic assessment of the whole range of the child's capabilities. This type of use is time-consuming but may be desirable in some contexts. The alternative approach is to use only one or two sections of the BAB with a child. The context in which this approach may be indicated is where the teacher has particular problems in understanding the child's functioning in limited areas and where a programme seems to be needed. We would ourselves suggest this more focussed approach as the one to choose because the basic purpose of the Battery is to plan for teaching rather than global assessment.

As we have indicated already the items are scored on to lattices. Each lattice is constructed in the same way. The order of items from the bottom to the top of the lattice reflects difficulty as revealed by the ease with which the children in the sample did the item. For example, in the Perceptual Problem Solving lattice (p. 166), two items, P1 - strikes at and knocks over obstacle - and P4 - obtains partially hidden object - are of equal difficulty. Item P22 at the right hand edge of the lattice is the next easiest item in the set, followed by P7 - object attached to cord is obtained. Items P27, P21 and P26 are the most difficult. As we already noted the coefficients of reproducibility show us how well items scale, in other words, the extent to which the difficulty measure applies to all of the children in the sample. High coefficients, like those shown for Constructive Play (0.95), Tracking (0.93), Search Strategies (0.91) and Visuo-Motor (0.91), suggest that there is a clear scale of difficulty. We cannot infer that this necessarily reflects a logical or developmental progression because the data are cross-sectional rather than longitudinal (parenthetically most so-called developmental schedules are also based on cross-sectional data). However we can make a reasonable presumption that high coefficients do indicate a logical progression in development, albeit possibly with some steps omitted, allowing us to teach toward a higher level target in the sequence. On the other hand lower coefficients, for example that for Exploratory Play (0.76), suggest either a looser logical structure to the section or a greater influence of individual differences.

We have said that the vertical organization of the lattices is completely empirically determined. However the left to right organisation is only partly determined by the data. It will be observed that the highest items in each of the stems in Figure 3 do arrange themselves in an ascending sequence and are thereby empirically determined. This is usually the case with the lattices in the BAB. However the collection of items on to the stems themselves is determined logically. The boxes indicating achievements, above the 'ridge line', represent achievements to which individual items appear logically related.

In constructing the lattices there were occasions, as with item P8 in Figure 3, when the pattern of individual responding suggested that two items, which are clearly logically linked and of more or less equivalent difficulty, were not clearly sequenced. For example, children scoring P7 scored on P8 *or* P9. Had there been a sequence we would have expected that P8 would normally have been scored correctly if the child had scored on P9. When this type of effect occurs we have indicated it by placing the items concerned in parallel.

Although the lattices reflect sequences we would not advocate their being used in a prescriptive way. As they stand now they represent *hypotheses* about the logical sequencing of development in particular areas. However we cannot know whether we have omitted critical steps and, consequently, it would be dangerous to suggest that having scored on one item and failed on the next in a sequence teaching *must* be directed at the type of task indicated by the failed item. We would suggest that teaching to the relevant task should be *seriously considered* but even the relatively detailed sequences which we have developed are likely to have gaps. Only experimentation through teaching will reveal where these gaps lie. We would suggest that this approach is the only one which is logically acceptable at the present time in our own case and in the case of so-called developmentally based programmes.

There is a further reason for avoiding a prescriptive use of the lattices. The precise interpretation of any success or failure must take into account other aspects of the child's functioning. This means that we need to see particular behaviours in context of problem behaviours, scores on other lattices, motor and sensory assessments and medical information on physical factors and conditions.

In practice we would suggest that the BAB may well serve its most useful purpose in helping the teacher to explore the child's behaviour and thereby aid understanding and stimulate ideas.

Programme development

Since the purpose of the Battery is to set up teaching programmes the assumption is made that the environment will lend itself to structured teaching using behavioural techniques (Foxen and McBrien, 1981). We would suggest that the BAB can best be employed in establishing target behaviours for teaching once basic objectives have been derived (Kiernan, 1980).

Decisions on priorities in teaching the severely mentally handicapped required a great deal of thought because of the interlocking nature of difficulties which children typically experience. Kiernan (1977, *see also* Kiernan, Jordan and Saunders, 1978) has suggested five areas which need to be considered together in evolving a programme. The five areas are educational blocks, rewards and interests, sensori-motor coordination, socialization and communication.

Educational blocks are defined as behaviours or disabilities which prevent the child from benefitting from education. They are various types of educational block and they may be highly idiosyncratic. An example of a block would be hand-biting which necessitated the child in question having his hands covered by gloves which are so thick that they interfere with sensori-motor play. Elimination of self-biting would be a top priority because, until the child is without gloves, his general education could not progress. Another example is of the child whose behaviour is aggressive or distasteful and who thereby jeopardizes the development of a satisfactory teaching relationship. Lack of adequate self-help skills may constitute a block to education in several ways. For example we have worked with children whose teaching day is almost entirely absorbed with being dressed, fed, toiletted and washed. Leaving aside the difficulties this creates for staff there is often very little time remaining in the day for any other activities.

The other main type of educational block stems from sensory or motor deficits. If these are present they need to be considered as priority areas for remedial treatment or dealt with through provision of aids which help to offset their effects. In the extreme cases of blindness, profound deafness or severe physical disability it seems reasonable to suggest that those cognitive functions which are likely to be affected should be developed through other means. Obvious examples are the use of sign language or symbol systems with the deaf child and use of mobility aids with the physically disabled.

Within the framework of the BAB the sections on Auditory Skills (5), Postural Control (6), Self-Help Skills (13) and Social Skills (11) all generate relevant information.

The second area for priority consideration is that of availability of *rewards* which can be used in the teaching situation, and *interests* which can be developed as settings for teaching (Section 1, Reinforcement and Experience). It is not uncommon to find children for whom there are very few usable rewards. However identification of rewards is essential if a programme is to progress. Similarly identifying a child's interests may be critical from several viewpoints. For example Kiernan and Jones (1982) report a symbol teaching programme in which a major difficulty was identifying topics about which the child could be motivated to communicate. Basically, although the child knew how to communicate she had little to say. In this type of case identification of preferred activities and interests becomes critical (Miller and Yoder, 1972).

The third area of focus suggested is the development of *sensori-motor coordination*. A comprehensive task analysis of a variety of areas of functioning shows that there is one key skill which without other skills can not be developed. This is the visually-directed reaching for and grasping of objects (Kiernan, 1981b). If this focal skill is not perfected it is hard to see how other skills which depend on it logically can emerge.

Data from the sections on Inspection (2), Tracking (3) and Visuo-Motor Skills (4) taken in context of information from Section 6, Postural Control, help to build up a usable picture.

Beyond the simple skill of visually-directed reaching the range and quality of the child's exploratory play will clearly be an important factor in his assimilation of information from his environment (Section 7, Exploratory Play). A restricted range of exploratory play behaviours is likely to act against the child. For example, if the child's exploratory play is restricted to mouthing objects, hitting them or throwing them without watching them, he will miss the point of many educational experiences because he will simply not engage his environment with a wide enough range of exploratory responses. Restricted exploratory play behaviour would suggest a priority of broadening the range of responses.

The skills involved in Search Strategies (9), including skills in object permanence, Perceptual Problem Solving (10) and Constructive Play (8) represent a higher level of consideration of the third area of focus.

The fourth priority area concerns *socialization*. We would suggest that if basic socialization is not shown then this should be a priority focus. If the child is to develop successfully he must accept and like other human beings. This enjoyment of the company of other children or, at the first level, attraction to adults, can be assessed partly through the sections on Reinforcement and Experience (1) and Social Behaviour (11).

Our fifth priority area concerns *communication*. We would suggest that the ability to communicate, even only at the level of communicating basic needs, is crucial. In fact it is arguable that the handicapped person is not really seen as 'human' until he or she can communicate. Recent developments in the use of sign and symbol systems have greatly simplified the problem of teaching communication skills. We would suggest that teaching communication skills should be a priority consideration even for children who may appear to be very profoundly handicapped.

The sections on Communication provide a fairly detailed background to programme development.

These five areas, dealing with educational blocks, rewards and interests, sensori-motor coordination, socialization and communication are clearly not exhaustive. For some children teaching self-help skills may not constitute the simple removal of an educational block but may represent a crucial social development for the child. In addition teaching such skills can involve developing other skills, such as sensori-motor skills and also the enhancement of socialization and communication. For this latter reason it seems sensible to see self-help skills as representing a different category of analysis in the curriculum. It is to this point that we now turn.

Core versus non-core: Skills versus activities

The distinction is often drawn between core and non-core aspects of the curriculum, most commonly in discussing normal education, but latterly, in discussions of special education. In special education distinctions emerge in terms of core aspects like teaching of communication, physical development, self-help skills, social education and cognitive skills as opposed to the non-core of art, pottery, music, dancing, sailing, and like activities. Kiernan (1982a) has argued that this type of distinction is inappropriately drawn since communication, motor coordination and other core aspects may have to be taught through highly personalized non-core aspects of the curriculum. In a case study Kiernan, Kavanagh and Bailey (1982) describe a programme in which the teaching of sensori-motor skills had to be initiated through the child drawing round a preferred toy with the reward of seeing the outline of the toy. Whilst this may be an extreme example it serves to make the point that we are not talking about core and non-core 'subjects' but about core *skills*, such as sensori-motor coordination or social skills, and that these skills may be elicited or taught in the context of a variety of *activities*, the subjects, which may be either traditionally core or non-core.

So far as the BAB is concerned the majority of sections deal specifically with what we would term skills. The exceptions are Section 1, Reinforcement and Experience, where motivational aspects of teaching and learning are covered, and Section 13 on Self-Help Skills. In the case of other sections we would clearly suggest inter-relations, for example, Constructive Play (8) assumes Visuo-Motor Skills (4) and Social Responsiveness (11) but in essence represents skills which are not committed to particular activities.

Activities stemming from BAB assessment

As we have just seen we would view BAB profiles as reflecting skill levels in a variety of areas. Since the general approach to testing suggests that optimal settings for testing are established and rewards are used to motivate subjects we would aim toward producing an optimal performance. These performances would then need to be explored in other teaching situations and built on through new teaching targets.

The sections of the BAB do not detail any specific teaching suggestions. There are now a large number of texts which link assessment to teaching suggestions. These include a range of books from North America (e.g. Bender and Valletutti, 1976; Bender, Valletutti and Bender, 1976), and several produced in the United Kingdom (e.g. Cunningham and Sloper, 1978; Jeffree and McConkey, 1976; Jeffree, McConkey and Hewson, 1977; Kiernan, 1981b; Kiernan, Jordan and Saunders, 1978). The Portage kit (Bluma, Shearer, Frohman and Hilliard, 1976) represents a further source of ideas. In a community-based project the optimal strategy with this collection of suggestions for activities proved to be the development of an amalgamated card-index system which referred the user to a variety of sources (Kiernan, 1982c).

In the current context we will not try to relate assessments to specific activities. However we will now examine the interpretation of scores on individual sections and, in the final part of this chapter, we will discuss the inter-relations of sections as they bear on programme development for Self-Help Skills and Communication.

Section 1. Reinforcement and Experience (pages 63 to 66)

This schedule is designed for completion with teachers and parents or other care-givers. It isolates potential rewards which may be used in a teaching programme. These may be grouped into rewards which are flexible and can be used in specific teaching situations and rewards which are more difficult to use in specific situations but may be used as back-up reinforcers in a token programme or for a child who is capable of understanding forward planning. In the first group might fall responses to questions R1, R3 (depending on the answer), R11, R13, R14 and possibly R15. Good rewards for use in specific teaching situations would be ones which could be easily manipulated by the teachers, in other words ones which could be presented easily in small 'doses', ones which the child finds highly rewarding and which do not pall rapidly, thereby avoiding satiation (cf. Kiernan, Jordan and Saunders, 1978). Rewarding experiences which may be used as back-up reinforcers may be identified through questions R3, R4, R6, R7, R8, R9, R11, R13, R14 and R15, again depending on the specific responses. Rewarding experiences which might be used as back-up rewards are characterized as being rather special events which, once entered into, cannot be simply switched off. For example simple social reward is a good teaching session reward because the teacher can stop attending or praising when the child stops behaving appropriately. However a car ride cannot be manipulated in this way. As a consequence although a car ride may be a substantial incentive it is poorly suited as a specific teaching reward.

Several questions in the section relate to the child's general experience of activities. They are designed to give a picture of his range of experience and also his reaction to those experiences. These include questions on playing outside (R4, R5), going to shops (R6, R9), going to various places by various forms of transport (R8, R7), going to see a variety of people (R10) and the ways in which he occupies himself at home and at school (R11, R12, R13, R14, R15).

This information may be used in several ways. It should allow a picture of the child's interest in people and events to be built up alongside a picture of problem behaviour and problem reactions. This can lead in several directions, including the development of specific programmes for the elimination of problem behaviours. These would sensibly be established only where it was clear that problem behaviours did not result from lack of skill, or from a general lack of social contact and deprivation of materials which might interest the child. Some environments in which problem behaviours develop constitute social and material deserts. For this reason it is important that we build up some picture of what the child does and can do before attacking the child's problem behaviours. If the problem behaviour results from 'boredom' elimination of the behaviour may well require enrichment of the social and material environment (Kiernan, 1974; Kiernan, Wright and Hawks, 1975). In building up this aspect of a programme data from this section should be taken in context of the over-all picture of the child's capabilities and especially sections concerning play (Exploratory Play, 7; Constructive Play, 8), Communication (12) and Social Behaviour (13) as well as descriptions of problem behaviour in Self-Help Skills (13) and from other knowledge of the child in his normal living environment.

The section on Reinforcement and Experience is of particular significance in the development of communication programmes. Easily manipulated rewards can be used in the initial phases of such a programme as 'topics' of communication. We will suggest later that the first steps in a programme should involve the child in using a word, speech sound, manual sign or symbol in 'asking' for an object or event, for example 'sweet' as a request to be given a sweet (Kiernan and Jones, 1982; Schaeffer, Musil and Kollinzas, 1980). The characteristics of a good reward and those of a valuable initial topic for communication overlap almost completely. Secondly, backup rewards which allow the child to do something special which he finds interesting can be used as topics for communication in a similar way, within the constraints of the child's general abilities. Regularly occurring events, fixed points in the day, and interesting or regularly occurring events, can be labelled within the programme as a move toward establishment of communicative functions such as description. The importance of isolating events which are significant or which act as turning points in the day has been suggested by several authors (e.g Konstantareas, Oxman and Webster, 1977; Schaeffer, Musil and Kollinzas, 1980).

Finally, knowledge of favourite activities and games (e.g. R5, R6, R8, R11, R12, R13, R14, R15) may provide a child-centred basis from which communication programmes can be developed. For some children the framework of a highly interesting game may be the only one through which communication can be developed (cf. Kiernan, Kavanagh and Bailey, 1982).

Section 2. Inspection (pages 67 to 70)

This section covers responses which develop early in normal development and which may be perfectly normal in the majority of handicapped children in the typical ESN(S) school. The responses covered include effective fixation, examination of two- and three-dimensional displays and visual exploration of the environment. The items are of central significance in outlining one critical set of skills without which other developments can not occur. The test procedures are best suited for children who are in general non-reactive and may even be thought to be blind. For this reason results need to be taken in context of physical examinations. For the children who are visually responsive and clearly not blind or visually defective many of the items will be inappropriate and may indeed be difficult to administer. In practice this tends to apply to all of the items except those relating to looking at books (I14, I15, I16), the observational items (I17, I18, I19 and I21) and, if the child is cooperative, convergence and divergence of the eyes (I10). We would suggest that other items be credited if the child is clearly capable.

Activities relating to this section are included in Cunningham and Sloper (1978), Jeffree, McConkey and Hewson (1977), Kiernan (1981b) and Kiernan, Jordan and Saunders (1978) amongst other sources.

Section 3. Tracking (pages 71 to 75)

This section covers tracking of visual stimuli with the eyes alone and through the head and eyes moving together, the prediction of movement of test objects and the prediction of movement of objects in play. The section builds on the results of Section 1 and again the data is of central significance in indicating pre-requisite skills for more complex behaviour. As with some of the items in Section 1 several of the items in Section 2 are difficult to administer to children or adults who clearly have good visual skills. In particular items T1 to T10, covering simple tracking with eyes and with eyes and head, may seem artificial to the capable child. If later items are scored or the child is clearly capable it may be safe to credit these items.

The later items in the section concern the use of tracking and the beginnings of problem solving and object permanence. Items examining relocation of objects which have been lost to central vision show a use of peripheral cues in identifying objects (T13, T14). Items requiring the child to adjust his position to continue seeing an object show the first levels of object permanence, of the awareness of continued existence of objects even when they are not visible (T11). The remaining items reflect further development of object permanence skills. T15 involves the child knowing that objects can be retained in vision if he moves. T12 and T17 suggest that the child does recognize that objects continue to exist when they are out of sight but only in situations where many other cues may be provided. T16 and T18 refer to the child's ability to predict movement when an object has disappeared behind a screen, and correct performance suggests the acquisition of object permanence skills in simple situations.

As can be seen from the ordering of items in the lattice (p. 159) demonstration of tracking skills and simple object permanence skills overlap in data from our study. This may suggest that the instrumental tracking skills develop in the context of the cognitive object permanence skills.

It is of interest that the play-related item, throwing and watching (T19), is the most difficult in the section. We will return to comment on the relation of test and observational items in considering Exploratory Play (Section 7).

Relevant activities are included in Kiernan (1981b), Kiernan, Jordan and Saunders (1978), Jeffree, McConkey and Hewson (1977) and Newson and Newson, (1979).

Section 4. Visuo- Motor (pages 76 to 79)

As we have already suggested this section reflects key behaviours without which a great deal of later development is logically inhibited. Earlier items in the section cover finger play and the child's reactions when his hands are touched or objects placed in them (V1 to V10). As with previous sections administration of the item may be problematic with more capable children and it may well be best to begin with item V11 in which the child's ability to reach and grasp is assessed, and to progress to item V17, the child moving to get an object. If the child is clearly capable earlier items may be credited although some reflect early stages of development beyond which the child will have progressed and which he may consequently 'fail' because the behaviours have been supplanted by more advanced ones.

The last three items in the section key into later sections but are included here as convenient extensions of testing of visuo-motor ability. Item V18 concerns the child's *awareness* of objects and supports but also his fine motor physical skills in picking up an object without disturbing the support. Items V19 and V20 examine the child's physical ability to position an object for visual examination and to rotate it in visual examination without dropping it.

In addition to the sources of suggested teaching activities which we have mentioned already (Cunningham and Sloper, 1978; Jeffree, McConkey and Hewson, 1977; Kiernan, 1981b; Kiernan, Jordan and Saunders, 1978; Newson and Newson, 1979) many useful suggestions are provided by Carr (1980) and Finnie (1974).

Section 5. Auditory (pages 80 to 83)

The first items in this section cover basic responsiveness to sound as assessed through simple behavioural indices (A1, A2). Data here needs to be interpreted in context of audiological examinations. The next group of items relate to audio-visual integration, whether the child responds to sound by turning to look at the sound's source (A3, A4). It is clearly possible that the child may hear normally but may have to learn to orient visually to sounds. In our experience this is seen most commonly in multiply handicapped children. The next two items (A5, A6) concern the child's responsiveness to human speech. Although this may indicate responsiveness or interest rather than understanding, the items are important in indicating the child's 'attitude' to speech sounds. The remaining test items (A7 to A11) all refer to sound-related play.

The interview items parallel test items.

The significance of basic responsiveness to sound and interest in sounds for development of concepts concerning objects and, in particular, for the understanding and use of communication, is obvious.

Activities concerned with the development of responsiveness to sounds are described by Jeffree and McConkey (1976) and Kiernan, Jordan and Saunders (1978) amongst others.

Section 6. Postural Control (pages 84 to 85)

This short section consists of interview items designed to assess head control, sitting and standing. The data from the section represent background information against which programmes can be planned. Full scale physical examination would be required in order to adequately assess less than total competence in postural control (see Finnie, 1974 and Levitt, 1977 for relevant exercises).

Section 7. Exploratory Play (pages 86 to 91)

As already indicated this section also covers behaviours which can be seen as key in the child's educational programme. Without adequate exploratory play skills the impact of provision of toys will be minimized.

The section is divided into six sub-sections on the lattice (p 163). Oral investigation may be seen as a relatively early and limited form of investigation. If the child's repertoire is restricted to this response it is worth considering training it out through substituting relatively more sophisticated responses such as banging, or shaking. In the group of children assessed it seemed clear that oral exploration had frequently ceased to be 'exploratory' as such, and was more akin to a mouthing and chewing habit.

Visual exploration and visuo-integration clearly constitute more sophisticated developments which have greater power in revealing critical features of the environment to the child. Techniques for encouraging or more formally teaching increasingly complex forms of these responses are described by Jeffree, McConkey and Hewson (1977), Kiernan (1981b) and Kiernan, Jordan and Saunders (1978).

Activities in the rolling and pushing group again reveal properties of the objects played with. They can be keyed into programmes of simple social interaction and coordinate with problem solving skills. Kiernan (1975) describes programmes in which simple social interaction between children was based on them being taught to roll a ball to one another (see also Kiernan, 1981b). Items involving pushing and pulling are precursors of skills concerned with the understanding of causality. It can be suggested that consistent experience of objects which are clearly attached to strings moving toward you when the string is pulled can form at least a partial basis for the understanding of the effects of one object on another.

The stem concerned with audio-visuo-motor integration represents a parallel development to visuo-motor stem. Here however the concern is with the integration of noise with the visuo-motor schema. Again apart from developing concepts of the objects, which these varied responses may allow, the behaviours can form a substrate for the understanding of cause and effect (see also Kiernan, 1981b).

As with prior examples there is some experimental data suggesting that responses in this group can be taught to children who do not already show them. For example Kiernan (1978) describes a set of studies in which squeezing and a turning response were taught to two severely mentally handicapped children. Generalization of the response from the training to test stimuli was demonstrated. Kiernan (1975) describes studies by Morales (1972) and Juvonen (1972) in which other exploratory responses were learned.

The development of the dropping-throwing stem implies several other schema already mentioned, including visuo-motor integration and the beginnings of an understanding of cause and effect.

It is of interest that this section has the lowest scale value of all the sections. This would suggest that the 'developmental' or logical sequences involved are far less prescribed than with other sections. So, although it is possible to draw out strands of logical connection, it would be dangerous to infer tight sequences. Indeed the current organization has some fairly arbitrary placements of individual items.

Section 8. Constructive Play (pages 92 to 96)

The section covers only three types of constructive play: play with a ball, drawing, and building with cubes. Clearly all three relate back to the development of inspection, tracking and visuo-motor integration as well as to aspects of exploratory play. All three represent ways in which the child may develop useful expressive skills (Kiernan, 1982a) but, in addition they provide further information on the child's processing of visuo-spatial information. The graphic skills involved in drawing may be eventually developed to a means of communication through some form of writing.

Section 9. Search Strategies (pages 97 to 102)

This section concerns the child's ability to conceptualize the continued existence of an object despite its disappearance from the direct visual field, object permanence, and the child's ability to mount a systematic search for an object which has been hidden. The section parallels Uzgiris and Hunt's Scale 1 (Uzgiris and Hunt, 1975).

Several of the items in this section are concerned with developments of tracking and were included in that section (SS1 to 6, 8 and 9). The achievement of object permanence is covered in the items on simple search. We would suggest that the key item is SS7 in which the child shows persistent search for an object which he has seen hidden by the Examiner.

It is often assumed that object permanence, once achieved, is a unitary concept, i.e. that the child achieves the idea of continued existence of objects for *all* objects simultaneously. We would suggest that this assumption is not necessarily true. It may well be that the child learns that particularly important people or objects continue to exist before the general rule is formulated. In fact the achievement of rule-related formulations may well not occur until language is well developed.

The stem concerned with complex search strategies relates to the concept of permanence of objects as used by Uzgiris and Hunt (1975). We have expressed it in terms of ability to search rather than to object permanence as such since it appears reasonable that the child may have a very well-established understanding of the continued existence of objects without being able to search effectively in the ways described. In other words we are suggesting two independent factors, permanence and skill in searching for hidden objects.

Finally it is interesting to see that evidence of object permanence in play appears to occur well after evidence appears in the test settings. It is often suggested that play be used as a means of assessing development of concepts such as object permanence. The present data indicates that reliance on observation in play may lead to underestimation of the child's abilities as shown by testing.

The broad implications of the achievements in this section bear on the development of communication, self-help skills and processes such as memory and planning. In particular it has been argued that object permanence is necessary before the child can learn to refer to objects or events which are not present. These considerations also refer to self-help skills.

Activities which may be used as a basis for teaching search strategies are included in the majority of the texts referred to already. Jeffree and McConkey (1976) and Kiernan (1981b) concern themselves in part with activities related to the development of memory.

Section 10. Perceptual Problem Solving (pages 103 to 109)

The items in this section cover several aspects of problem solving from simple negotiation of objects to strategies for complex handling of objects. Several of the items parallel those in the Uzgiris and Hunt Scale II (Uzgiris and Hunt, 1975).

The first two stems on the lattice reflect the child's ability to handle very simple situations in which obstacles have to be moved for the child to obtain the incentive. The next two stems reflect the development of understanding of means-end relationships or cause and effect. One stem reflects Piagetian tasks and really deals with understanding of means-end relationships involving objects and the second means-end relationships concerning other human beings. We would suggest that this distinction could be very important. There seems to be no reason why understanding of the two types of situation should not appear - or be developed - independently of each other. The emergence of understanding of means-end relationships has been seen as a crucial step in the evolution of communication skills. Until the child understands that his behaviour can affect the behaviour of another person he cannot be sensibly said to be communicating. Whether the child needs to show understanding of means-end relationships *before* he can communicate or whether he can learn about means-end *within* a communication teaching situation is a moot point. It may well be that the child learns that he can affect other people predictably in such situations.

The remaining stems in the lattice concern methods of solving other types of perceptual problem. The items suggest a number of possible activities. Others are included in Jeffree and McConkey (1976), Kiernan (1981b) who discusses other types of cause and effect situations, and Kiernan, Jordan and Saunders (1978).

Section 11. Social (pages 110 to 114)

This section provides a relatively brief series of questions concerning basic social responsiveness and responsiveness to his own image. The items are largely drawn from other sections. The section can provide information to complement other orientations in programme development.

The remaining sections in the BAB cover Communication (12) and Self-Help Skills (13). We will deal with these sections in a rather different way from that used in commenting on other sections. In these cases we will interpret the sections in context of the other sections in the BAB, and in the context of development of teaching programmes.

Section 12. Communication (pages 115 to 140)

As we have already suggested a component concerned with communication should be seen as a critical element in any individual programme. We will define a communicative act as a response which the child makes *with the intention* of affecting another person. The concept of intention can be realized in various ways. For example a child who is crying can sensibly be said to be trying to communicate, if when the adult responds, he stops crying before the cause of the crying has been removed. In other words the purpose or intent of the crying was to attract attention and once that is achieved it stops. Communication involves a feedback loop in which the child shows himself to be aware of the other person's response and, as he becomes more sophisticated, aware of the particular *quality* of response which he wished to produce in the person he is communicating with.

This formulation implies a variety of features of communication. In order to communicate the child needs the basic 'idea' of communication. In addition he needs to have a means of communicating either through sounds or other means. He also has to have something to say before he will communicate. Finally he needs the motivation to communicate which will be conditioned by past responses of the environment to his attempts to communicate (Miller and Yoder, 1972).

Within the framework of the BAB we have already suggested that the assessment of Reinforcement and Experience bears centrally on the development of a communication programme. We would suggest that the 'idea' of communication can best be established by teaching the child that, through specific responses, he can obtain a specific set of rewards (cf. Kiernan, Jordan and Saunders, 1978; Schaeffer, Musil and Kollinzas, 1980). The steps in establishing such a programme are firstly, to isolate rewards which are high-value rewards and which can be easily manipulated. They can then be given to the child in a setting in which the child is, if necessary, prompted to make a selected response which is then immediately reinforced by a particular reward. When this response is established a second response is taught leading to a second reward, and so on. This approach builds up a set of responses which are discriminated in terms of their outcome (Kiernan and Jones, 1982).

In terms of the general model, this approach uses requests for rewards as the basic message content. The child is taught the equivalent of 'I want...'. The way of asking is specifically shaped. The motivation to communicate is initiated and maintained by consistent reward, initially in a structured setting.

The attraction of this approach is that it makes few assumptions about the skills which a child might bring to a situation. The approach requires little in the way of understanding of speech or other modes through which communication may occur. Two other 'pre-requisites', object permanence and means-end awareness, may not be necessary either. Within the initial approach described there is no need to expect the child to be aware of the continued existence of objects, since the basic communicative act can be accomplished without such knowledge. Secondly, as we have already implied, the understanding of basic social means-end relationships may actually be learned in settings like the one described.

We are not suggesting that object permanence and understanding of means-end are irrelevant. Our central point is that they are not *necessary* before a communication programme can begin and that such a programme may in fact help their development.

We would argue that other skills which the child brings to the programme have to be carefully considered in order to establish the optimal form of a communication programme.

The Communication Interview and the tests of Imitative and Expressive and Receptive Abilities all bear on the form of programme development in the context of performance on other sections in the BAB.

The assessment of receptive abilities covers several areas (Lattice page 168). Data on hearing and listening needs to be taken in conjunction with data from the Auditory Skills section and audiological and related assessments. The next three stems relate to the understanding of need-related gestures, words, and non-fade symbols (pictures or pictograms). It is clear that these stems relate to the possible use of signs, speech or symbols in a formal programme. The next two stems concern the more sophisticated communicative function, naming. The final stem relates to other communicative functions up to the use of prepositions.

At a simple level it can be suggested that, if the child can understand a communicative function like asking, describing or those embodied in simple phrases, then he can be considered a candidate for an expressive programme teaching that function. However, the converse may not hold. If a child does not understand need-related messages we cannot assume that he cannot be taught to use them. Current research shows that receptive and expressive skills can and do develop independently. Certainly, acquisition of receptive skills does not always predate acquisition of expressive skills.

The Receptive Test (page 127) can be used in two ways. First of all we can assess the child's knowledge of names of objects. Secondly, even if the child does not succeed on the Test phase, the Pre-Training data can give an indication of whether, with teaching, the child can begin to learn names for objects.

The Development of Sounds and Imitation sections of the Interview (page 119) and related Tests helps to build up a further picture of basic skills. Production of speech sounds is clearly necessary if speech is to develop. However, the fact that the child produces a variety of sounds does not necessarily mean that sounds will be used communicatively. In fact we can go beyond this. The fact that a child has normal speech musculature, as indexed by normal eating, does not necessarily mean that speech sounds will be produced. Consequently speech-sound development needs to be assessed as a tool skill.

The assessment suggested here can sensibly be complemented by a phonological analysis of speech sounds. This may then lead to a specific programme to develop new speech sounds.

Motor and Verbal imitative skills assessed through the Interview (pages 130 to 135) and relevant tests are, similarly, necessary but not sufficient skills for communication. Development of sign involves motor imitation and development of speech verbal imitation, but, as with speech sounds, the ability to imitate does not mean that the child will use the responses which are imitated in a communicative way. The lay-out of the lattice suggests the levels at which the Motor and Verbal Imitation Test results will be relevant. However, as with the Vocublary Tests, the Pre-training sections can give the user information on whether the child is suitable for an imitation training programme.

The Motor Imitation Test can be used to explore the child's skills in context of possible placement in a sign language programme. Poor performance on the Pre-training or List 1 section would suggest a need to enhance these skills as such before placement in such a programme. However such a decision would need to be taken only after also looking at performance on the Sign Imitation Test (see below). List 2 contains items which cover both object- and body-oriented imitation. Some children, whose object-related imitation is good, have great difficulty with body-oriented imitation. Such a pattern may contra-indicate use of sign with those children suggesting instead that symbols and speech should be emphasized.

The Verbal Imitation Test results need to be taken into account in framing any type of communication programme. We would suggest that an adequate programme *must* contain a speech related component if the child has minimal physical skills (if he can eat normally and has normal breathing). If the child scores poorly on verbal imitation, signs or symbols may be selected as the initial means of communication but a verbal imitation teaching programme should be included as a component of the programme in order that speech sound production can be included as a communicative mode when the child learns to imitate effectively. Kiernan, Jordan and Saunders (1978) and Schaeffer, Musil and Kollinzas (1980) describe methods for imitation training.

We would suggest that the Sign Imitation Test (page 135) should be used mainly for children who are in sign language programmes as a means of assessing their progress in identifying crucial features of hand postures and other aspects of signs. The data gathered in development of the procedure suggested two types of error. Some children committed errors in which they selected and imitated one feature of the posture, for example the extended index finger of the Index hand, but erred in not folding the other fingers into a fist. Other children erred in producing a posture which, overall, looked like the required posture but which was incorrect in form. So, for example, an Index Hand was imitated by extending the thumb or fourth finger from the fist. Other errors involved failure to match the number of fingers extended and, in particular, to match the thumb position. Identification of errors should sensibly lead to remedial 'articulation' training. This might take several forms including the selection of signs which exemplify the poorly articulated signs or teaching the child 'games' in which he is asked to identify and match poorly articulated hand shapes (Jones and Kiernan, 1981).

The assessment of expressive abilities through the Communication Interview (page 120) and the Expressive Vocabulary Test (page 122) is organized on parallel lines to the assessment of receptive abilities. We would suggest that assessment of whether the child has needs, preferences or interests as well as basic responsiveness to adults is fundamental to the development of communication skills. If there are no needs and preferences then the child has little or nothing to say and programmes to establish such needs and interests need to be set up (Kiernan, 1981b; Kiernan, Jordan and Saunders, 1978). Lack of basic responsiveness to adults may not contra-indicate the development of a communication programme but would certainly suggest the need for an increase in rewarding social contact.

The next four stems on the lattice, referring to asking through manipulation, pointing to objects or pictures, gestures, and sounds, relate to the primary communicative function, asking, and may well have been developed by the child prior to any formal teaching. Clearly, note needs to be taken of the mode which has been spontaneously selected in deciding on the mode to be used in teaching.

The next stem, concerned with the use of single 'words', refers to spoken words, signs and symbols when used on their own. The term 'word' is used here to cover any of the various modes. Three functions are covered here, recurrence, negation and description. We are not suggesting that a formal language is needed to express these functions. Certainly negation and recurrence can be expressed through other modes.

The last stem relates to various uses of 'phrases', two-item utterances which may be expressed in spoken words, signs or in symbols.

The Choice Amongst Augmentative Systems. We would make two assumptions about communication programmes. The first is that the end point of any programme should be the development of speech. Even if it is not felt to be feasible, provided the child or adult has the basic equipment necessary for speech production, speech would sensibly be the aim. The reason for this firm statement is that speech is used as *the* means of communication in society and if the child is to gain, receptively and expressively, from his speech environment, he must be able to key into it. If the child has, through physical damage, lost the potential for speech the programme should be aimed at competence in a speech-equivalent, use of written words, either as such or as symbols, or the ability to write spoken English.

The second assumption is that the child should be provided with a means of communication as early as possible in order to avoid frustration and to begin to develop human contact and interaction. Since so much learning stems from the interaction with other human beings it seems critical that socialization and communication are given high priority in programming.

These assumptions condition our approach to the selection of the mode for communication teaching. We would suggest that the mode chosen should be the one which the child can learn to use most rapidly. In practice, for reasons which should become clear shortly, this may well mean the use of non-fade symbols. However we would also suggest that use should be made of more than one mode both as a short-term teaching assessment strategy and as a long-term strategy for capitalizing on the strengths of the various systems.

Hollis and Carrier (1978) have pointed out that we need to identify a functional communication channel before intervention can be attempted. This involves deciding on the sensory input mode which may be visual, auditory, tactile or olfactory, the conceptual level at which the intervention is to occur, starting for example with imitative responses by the child, and the output mode, which may involve fine or gross motor movements, signing, writing or speech.

Within our assessment framework the different systems will place different demands in terms of the characteristics of the channel. We turn now to a consideraion of these characteristics for different modes.

Symbols.   The central characteristic of symbol systems as defined here is that the elements used in communication do not disappear over time. As opposed to a spoken word or manual sign a symbol persists. What produces variation is the user's indication of the chosen symbol. Secondly the user's response can be very simple involving anything from placing a finger or hand on the relevant symbol to blowing on a paddle in order to move an index light (see Silverman, 1980 for a full discussion of responses which can be used as index responses).

Beyond this, symbol systems are extremely diverse. On the input side symbols can be either visual or tactile, for the blind or partially-sighted raised, three-dimensional or texturally differentiated symbols can be used. Visually-based symbols can represent their referents in a wide variety of ways from direct matching of the referent by a three-dimensional equivalent, either at full size or reduced size, through colour pictures of particular objects, black and white pictures, line drawings, pictograms, abstracted representations, to ideograms and finally to purely abstract symbols (Fristoe and Lloyd, 1979).

There is very little research bearing on the question of choice of level of representation. Kuntz, Carrier and Hollis (1979) have shown that association of strongly representational symbols with their referents is more rapid than association of abstract symbols. They also suggest that transfer from symbols to words is more rapid with abstract symbols but their data is not easy to interpret. Certainly it would seem reasonable to assume that the more directly representational the symbol is, the more likely the child is to associate symbol with referent. Given this assumption the closer the representation is to the object at the beginning of teaching the more rapidly one would expect communication skills to be established.

Beyond a very simple level of symbol-concept correspondence it is necessary to introduce organizing rules into a symbol system. Systems such as Blissymbols, (Bliss, 1965), Rebus (Clark and Woodcock, 1976), Sigsymbols (Cregan, 1982) and written words all have their rule sets which allow them to represent nouns, verbs, prepositions and other elements in communication in a more or less predictable way. Initial choice of level of representaiton may sensibly relate to the form of the symbol system which is seen as the ultimate aim of the programme.

The non-fade nature of visual or tactile symbols bestows two further advantages. First of all it is only necessary for the user to *recognize* and indicate a symbol from amongst an array in order to be able to communicate. Signs and spoken words require the user to *recall* the item. Clearly recall is normally a more complex and more difficult process than recognition and consequently non-fade symbols begin with a built-in advantage over other modes.

Secondly symbols may allow the user to acquire linguistic rules more rapidly than signs or spoken words. In using symbols the process of forming a sentence can be split down into two operations, selecting the elements and arranging them in the appropriate sequence. House, Hanley and Magid (1980) describe this two-stage process in their subjects' performance in a 'reading' task. After teaching four mentally handicapped adults to use a 'logographic' system to describe a series of pictures, House and her colleagues found that, faced with a new picture, their students first of all sorted out the five symbols needed to describe the picture (e.g. 'woman puts hat in box') and then put them in the correct sequence. The order in which the symbols were initially selected differed from student to student but, for individuals, was reasonably predictable. House and her colleagues point out that, overall, initial selection was done in terms of semantic salience, rather than in sentence order. As opposed to the situation with symbols, selection and arrangement must be performed simultaneously when subjects are using signs or words.

We would suggest that teachers should entertain the possibility of teaching children to use both signs or speech *and* corresponding symbols on a continuing basis as a means of providing an effective means of teaching linguistic rules once the transition to multi-element utterances is made.

The behaviour which the child should be showing in order to be entered into a symbol programme will clearly depend on the nature of the programme. The simplest level of programme would place few requirements. If we assume that the child is simply going to learn to select a symbol corresponding to a need or wish for an object which is present, for example, one of several edible incentives presented in full view, then requirements are minimal. Such a programme would require identification of at least two usable edible rewards (Reinforcement and Experience), ability in Inspection and some competence in Tracking and a minimal degree of Visuo-Motor coordination. This would allow the child to perceive the reward and 'symbol' and to indicate the symbol by touching. Such a programme would not require any competence in object permanence or in understanding of means-end relationships since the object is in full view and the response can be physically prompted in the first instance. In fact we would suggest that such competences may be learned in the course of a programme of this sort rather than being pre-requisites. Nor would the child need to show competence in processing Auditory input. The stimuli used could be purely visual.

More complex symbols will require other abilities, as would the use of speech as an input mode. However the particular strength of symbol programmes is their ability to place minimal requirements on users in the first stages.

Signs. Many of the considerations applying to the use of symbols also hold with the use of signs. Signs can be simplified for the beginning stages of programmes. Initial stages of the programme can be used to establish communication in the 'asking' situation even when object permanence and means-end relationship understanding is in doubt. Similarly it is possible to physically prompt the child to use signs, although prompting will clearly be more difficult than the prompting of pointing or touching in symbol use. However signs do require the user to recall the form of the sign and to develop an understanding of the 'articulatory' structure of signs (Brennan, Colville and Lawson, 1980; Wilbur, 1979).

In terms of the BAB assessment a minimal programme requires Inspection, Tracking and a degree of motor control. Beyond this level factors such as ability to imitate (Motor Imitation), social responsiveness (Social) and object permanence and understanding of means-end relationships rapidly become relevant. It may well be that the substantial individual differences observed in signing programmes relate to the sophistication of the child on these various dimensions (Curcio, 1978; Kiernan, 1982b; Kiernan, Reid and Jones, 1982). The BAB assessments should allow their users to identify these levels of sophistication. We would hypothesize that the greater the level of skill shown on these scales the more readily the child would learn to use sign.

As already noted the Sign Imitation Test (pages 135 to 140) is designed specifically to assess the child's ability to imitate signs used in various systems. The Test may be used at the beginning of sign teaching to assess likely initial success. As already noted, if the student can imitate three hand postures, Flat Hand, Fist Hand and Index Finger Hand, he will be able to imitate a substantial proportion of commonly-used signs. If the child cannot imitate these postures the construction of the early stages of teaching should differentiate the basic postures in terms of meaning for the child. This may well involve the invention of the signs to exemplify the postures (Kiernan, Reid and Jones, 1982). The same basic strategy may be used with more complex postures.

As we have already noted, particular attention may need to be paid to the child's ability to imitate body-oriented as opposed to object-oriented responses in the Motor Imitation Test. In our experience some children find especial difficulty with body-oriented imitation. This may well relate to poor performance in sign programmes (see also the Social section on interest in reflected images).

Spoken Words. Of the three types of systems spoken words place the greatest requirements on the child. Before words can be used communicatively the child should have established needs or interests, be able to hear and understand speech at least minimally, to be able to imitate verbally again at least minimally, and be able to produce at least some speech sounds. Several aspects of this array of skills may be difficult to assess (e.g. hearing and understanding of speech). Other aspects are difficult to teach if they are not already present. For example it is difficult to teach the child to produce speech sounds. This leads to problems with verbal imitation and attaching meaning to sounds because the teaching situation is typically difficult to control.

For the child with intact speech production mechanisms the only usable steps in programming are to teach verbal imitation, if possible within a situation where different speech sounds are differentially rewarded (cf. Schaeffer, Musil and Kollinzas, 1980). Clearly the sequence of introduction of speech sounds into the imitation programme would sensibly follow a pattern reflecting the development of articulation skills (cf. Ingram, 1976; McReynolds and Engmann, 1975).

Combined Use of Modes. Several programmes have now been published which combine the use of modes. Alpert (1980) and Kiernan and Jones (1982) combine sign and symbol use with a view to identifying the most appropriate mode for the child. Schaeffer, Musil and Kollinzas (1980) combine sign and speech. In this programme, speech is introduced into the communication setting only when a reasonable level of verbal imitation is achieved. Evidence from a number of studies indicates the importance of *specific* verbal imitation training for non-speaking children (Kiernan, 1982b). Simply using

spoken words with signs (Total Communication) does not guarantee
the acquisition of speech within a sign programme if the child does not
have verbal imitation skills prior to the programme.

The revised techniques for assessing Expressive and Receptive
Vocabulary (pages 122 to 130) have been designed to allow the user to
identify which of the various possible aspects of the stimulus complex
used in Total Communication the child is responding to. Studies by
Carr and others have shown that different children respond to
different aspects of input (Carr, 1979; Churchill, 1978; Kiernan,
1982b). The knowledge that the child is, for example, responding with
sign purely to the sight of an object rather than its spoken name can
give additional insight into the child's abilities and lead to the
development of programmes to enhance understanding of speech.
Level of Communication.   We have talked so far mainly about the
initial levels of communication, asking for rewards, which a child may
show and which can be used in teaching. Developmental studies
suggest that further levels include 'drawing attention', basic
descriptive statements, negation and recurrence. Programming for
development beyond the one-word level can clearly be based on those
functions shown at the one-word level in the Expressive Abilities
lattice (page 170). We would suggest that choice of format to be taught
should depend on the child's communication needs rather than on
fixed rules (Kiernan, 1982d). Robson, Jones and Storey (1980) have
developed procedures for identifying goals for programmes beyond
the one-word level within the context of an excellent practical minicourse (Project TASS).

Self-Help Skills

Self-help skills often form part of the 'core' curriculum for the child
in ESN(S) schools. We may again suggest minimal requirements for the
acquisition of such skills.

At the simplest level of functioning where the child is fed, washed,
dressed and cleaned only passive participation is necessary. Food may
indeed be consumed on a purely reflex basis. Beyond this minimal
level any learning must be mediated through the child's needs and
preferences. Development of feeding skills is necessarily based on the
child's enjoyment of food. Toilet training would ideally be based on
the child's feelings of discomfort at being wet or dirty, probably
coupled with adult disapproval of soiling (Azrin and Foxx, 1974).

The difficulty with some self-help skills areas, especially dressing and washing, is that it is hard to see what intrinsic rewards they have for the child in the early levels of his development. Until the child has an appreciation of the association of activities over time he cannot be reinforced for dressing by being taken out to the shops or some other enjoyable activity. Under these circumstances there is a need to rely on artificial rewards in order to teach these skills.

As with the various types of communication skills several abilities would appear to be basic to the acquisition of self-help skills. Visuo-motor skills are clearly central, coupled with Inspection and Tracking skills or their non-visual equivalent. The skills shown in Exploratory Play and Constructive Play may give a better index of sophistication in object handling. Auditory skills, or their equivalent in signs or symbols, are clearly critical if adult teaching is to be effective. Postural control needs to be considered in programme development. The attainment of object permanence and of skills in search and perceptual problem solving may be critical for some skills, for example independent toileting.

Overall we would suggest that the relation of basic skills to achievement of success in self-help skills programmes is similar to that which holds for communication. We can, with care, key the programme to a fairly limited level of functioning. However, if the programme is to lead the child to normal development of skills complex processes are clearly assumed.

Concluding comment

In this chapter we have tried to indicate how we would see the BAB being used in practice. Our central premise is that programming for teaching needs to be based on a consideration of individual profiles. There is little mileage in trying to produce fixed prescriptive programmes. We have offered suggestions on how responses may be interpreted and of the pre-requisites for particular skills. Overall, although there are a few key areas and concepts, we would suggest that the keynote of programming should be flexibility and ingenuity in working toward programme goals. There are more ways of skinning a cat than boiling it in oil and more ways of achieving development than prescriptive programmes can ever conceive.

Behaviour Assessment Battery

1. REINFORCEMENT AND EXPERIENCE

This section is designed to obtain information on potential reinforcers and the reinforcement strategies used by the parents, nurses or teachers. The section also asks about the child's experience and preferred activities in a free setting.

Schedule

We are trying to find out the things that each child likes. This information is most helpful in designing training programmes. Most children are fond of sweets, perhaps we could make a list of those liked by . . . . , and say which he is most fond of. (Then cover each of the areas listed below.)

R1 *Sweets*
e.g. Smarties, chocolate buttons.

(a)　1. _____
　　 2. _____
　　 3. _____
　　 4. _____
　　 5. _____
　　 6. _____

Drinks

(c)　1. _____
　　 2. _____
　　 3. _____
　　 4. _____
　　 5. _____
　　 6. _____

Being Spoken to
e.g. Praise, nursery rhymes, songs

(e)　1. _____
　　 2. _____
　　 3. _____
　　 4. _____
　　 5. _____
　　 6. _____

Other Foods
e.g. Crisps, bread and butter, biscuits

(b)　1. _____
　　 2. _____
　　 3. _____
　　 4. _____
　　 5. _____
　　 6. _____

Touching and Tickling

(d)　1. _____
　　 2. _____
　　 3. _____
　　 4. _____
　　 5. _____
　　 6. _____

Other
e.g. Music, TV (which programmes), toys

(f)　1. _____
　　 2. _____
　　 3. _____
　　 4. _____
　　 5. _____
　　 6. _____

R2   If he is upset and crying what do you find the best way of calming
      him down most quickly? _____

R3   If he has been especially good or has done something very well
      how do you usually reward him? _____

R4   Does he play outside? When did he last do this?
      Today _____Yesterday _____This week_____
      During past 4 weeks _____

R5   Does he like playing outside?   _____
      Goes out on own accord   _____
      Indicates desire to go out   _____
      Only keen to go out when accompanied   _____
      Reluctant to go out   _____
      Cries or actively resists going out   _____
      Appears not to notice whether in or out   _____

R6   How often is he taken out to the shops or on a trip?
      Most days _____ More than twice a week_____Once a week _____
      At least once a month _____

R7   When was he last taken out in a car, taxi, bus, etc. (when one clarified
      go on to others)

	Past week	Past month	Past year
Car			
Taxi			
Bus			
Train			
Tube			

R8   Does he like going out in a car, etc.? Has he gone on any of the
      following:

	Past week	Past month	Past year
Walk in the town			
Walk in the country			
Seaside			
Picnic			
Zoo			
Circus			

Farm _____ _____ _____
Cinema _____ _____ _____
Theatre _____ _____ _____

R9 Has he been shopping with an adult over the last
Day _____ Week _____ Month _____
Does he enjoy shopping?
Are there any problems with shopping?
(Identify problems as clearly as possible.)
Do these problems limit you going out or taking him to the
shops?

R10 Has he been to see any of the following?

	Past week	Past month	Past year
Hairdresser			
Dentist			
Physiotherapist			
Optician			
Speech therapist			
Psychologist			
Doctor			
Teacher			

How does he react? (Get full picture if possible.)

R11 Does he watch or listen to:

	Past week	Past month	Past year
Radio			
TV			
Records			
Films			

R12 Does he watch or help with any of the following?

	Past week	Past month	Past year
Food preparation			
Housework			
Gardening			
Other jobs			

What does he do? _____

R13 Does he look at books, pictures, etc.? _____
     What does he look at? _____

R14 What three toys does he play with most frequently?

     1. _____   _____
     2. _____   _____
     3. _____   _____

Comments.

R15 What three games does he play most frequently?

     Alone
     1. _____   _____
     2. _____   _____
     3. _____   _____

     With children
     1. _____   _____
     2. _____   _____
     3. _____   _____

     With mother or teacher or nurse
     1. _____   _____
     2. _____   _____
     3. _____   _____

2.INSPECTION

This section covers Defensive Reactions, Effective Fixation, the Examination of Three and Two Dimensional Displays and Explor-ation of the Environment. Items 1-16 and 20 are test items. Items 17-19 and 21 are observational items which may be recorded first or during the test session.

Equipment

Small torch, 10.2 cms red cubes in box, red sweets (about 1.5 cms diameter). Six small toys, e.g. model animals about 12 cms high. Three toy cars. Objects with silent movement are very useful, e.g. a White Stimulus a bundle of coloured feathers and tinsel (White, 1970), Picture Book. Ten sheets A4 plain paper, nylon or felt tipped pens or crayons. Colour discs.

Test items

I1 *Criterion Behaviour* — The child blinks at a hand passing over his eyes.

 Presentation — The child should be looking at a point away from E's hand so that its appearance is unexpected.

I2 *Criterion Behaviour* — The child blinks, rapidly turns his head, or takes other evasive action when an object rapidly approaches his eyes.

 Presentation — A small bright coloured object, e.g. the lighted torch is moved rapidly towards the child's eyes.

I3 *Criterion Behaviour* — The child visually fixates a stationary object but the fixation is only maintained with frequent minor readaptive movements of the eyes.

 Presentation — A small torch is held stationary at the centre of the visual field approximately 50 centimetres from the child's face. This should be alternated with presentations in the right and left periphery of the visual field. Each presen-tation for around 10 seconds, up to six presentations.

I4 *Criterion Behaviour* — The facial expression and body move-ments which accompany the visual fixation indicate 'attention', 'effort', 'really looking' as opposed to 'vague contemplation'.

 Presentation — As in I3

I5   *Criterion Behaviour* — The child responds to luminous or non-luminous object held stationary in his visual field by changes in facial expression. His fixation need not be effective in order for him to score.

Presentation — The child looks at a torch or lighted window, or at an area of bright colour or object. Try a selection of objects, the child may well only look at preferred objects.

I6   *Criterion Behaviour* — The child fixates a stationary object without difficulty and the gaze is held steady.

Presentation — As in I3.

I7   *Criterion Behaviour* — When a cube is placed upon the table before the child and his attention is drawn to it, he fixates it for up to three seconds.

Presentation — The red cube is moved slowly in from the periphery of the child's visual field. It is then tapped down upon the table three times and left there. Examiner points to the brick saying 'see the brick', etc., for about 10 seconds.

I8   *Criterion Behaviour* — When a cube is placed upon the table before the child and his attention is drawn to it, he fixates it for at least three seconds.

Presentation — As in I7.

I9   *Criterion Behaviour* — The child fixates without difficulty a red sweet c. 1.5 cms placed on a plain white surface. The gaze is held steady.

Presentation — The child's attention should be attracted to the sweet which is put about 40 cms in front of him. The child should fixate it for at least three seconds (or reach and grasp it whilst fixating) to score.

I10   *Criterion Behaviour* — The child looks at an object and maintains fixation as it is slowly moved closer to and away from him. The child's eyes converge and diverge.

Presentation — The object, the torch, cube or toy, is presented at a distance of 40 cms in the centre of the child's visual field.

Once the child is looking at the object it is slowly moved closer to the child. It is stopped at 15 cms and is then moved slowly away again.

I11   *Criterion Behaviour* — The child will turn and look at an object when it is brought in from the periphery of his visual field.

Presentation — The child should be looking at an object presented at the centre of his visual field. The object shown should be one which will attract and hold the child's attention for a few seconds but not a highly valued incentive likely to render him unresponsive to other visual input. The child should be looking at but not manipulating the object. A second object is then slowly moved into the peripheral areas of his visual field. This object should be brought progressively nearer to the centre of his visual field until the child looks at it. Repeat up to six trials if necessary. Make sure that the objects are interesting to the child and that his visual attention is not cued by following the arm manipulating the second object.

I12   *Criterion Behaviour* — When the child is presented with two objects successively, the second entering the visual field once the first has been fixated, both objects remaining stationary after presentation, the child alternates his glance between the two objects.

Presentation — The first of two objects is held slightly to one side of the centre of the child's mid-line. Once it has been fixated the second object is introduced around 20 cms from the first at the other side of the mid-line. Both objects are held stationary for about 20 seconds. Use objects which interest the child.

I13
(S2)   *Criterion Behaviour* — The child inspects the examiner's face, looking from one feature to another.

Presentation — Examiner should position his face some 40 cms from the child's face in his direct line of vision whilst smiling and talking to the child.

I14   *Criterion Behaviour* — The child looks at a picture, rather than at a book as a whole, before using the book inappropriately or losing interest. The child should visually fixate a picture for 5 seconds plus to score.

Presentation — The child is given a sturdy book with simple coloured pictures. He is encouraged to look at the pictures. Keep trying for at least 30 seconds.

I15
(CP12)

Criterion Behaviour — When examiner draws and scribbles on a piece of paper which is placed directly in front of the child at a distance of about 40 cms, the child watches for 10 seconds or more.

Presentation — Examiner draws a simple outline shape, e.g. a cat, whilst encouraging the child to attend by tapping the pen, vigorous filling in the outline, or verbal description.

I16
(S8)

Criterion Behaviour — The child maintains his interest in a book when with an adult for at least *one minute*.

Presentation — As in I14.

I20

Criterion Behaviour — The child on looking at an object (particularly a familiar object), responds with a definite smile. The smile *may* be social but a toy may evoke the same response.

Presentation — Objects which are likely to resemble toys familiar to the child or toys which he knows (teddy bear, car, doll, etc.) are shown to him. If the response is noted in other situations it should be scored.

Observational items

When the child is taken into an unfamiliar environment (the assessment room) he responds in one or more of the following ways during the first four minutes.

I17   Sits passively, visual exploration without head movements.

I18   Sits, moves head to increase range of vision.

I19   Explores novel environment without leaving seat, reaches round, etc.

I21   Leaves seat to explore.

3. TRACKING

This section covers tracking with the eyes, and eyes and head, visual prediction of movement of test objects and visual prediction of movement in play.

Equipment

Small torch, six small toys, three toy cars, pull-along toy, ball, soft pad, two opaque screens, each 20 cms by 20 cms, cord to suspend objects. The child should be seated or propped. Care should be taken to ensure that children who lack adequate head control are given a great deal of support. Visual tracking will be adversely affected if this is not ensured.

Test items

T1   *Criterion Behaviour* — The child's eyes or head make small sideways movements in the same direction as a slowly moving object which passes through the centre of his visual field.

        Presentation — The object, e.g. a torch or small toy, is slowly moved to and fro in the horizontal plane, so that it passes through the centre of the child's visual field. The object should initially be presented at a distance of 40 cms. The presentation distance should be varied if the response does not appear immediately.

T2   *Criterion Behaviour* — The child's *eyes* follow a moving object through all or most of the half-circle of its movement from one side of the child to the other (horizontal movement).

        Presentation — As in T1.

T3   *Criterion Behaviour* — The child's *eyes* follow a moving object through the major part of its vertical trajectory.

        Presentation — As in T1 except that the object is moved slowly up and down.

T4   *Criterion Behaviour* — The child's *eyes* follow a moving object through the major part of the upper and lower of its circular trajectory without moving the head. (Many children find the transition points between the upper and lower halves of the circle difficult to follow smoothly. The way in which the child copes with this transition may be noted separately.)

Presentation — As in T1 except that the object is moved 15 cms horizontally from the mid-point before beginning to trace a circle of approximately 30 cms diameter. The circle should be traced slowly two or three times.

T5 *Criterion Behaviour* — The child's *eyes* follow a moving object through the major part of its irregular trajectory.

Presentation — As in T1 the irregular trajectory starts at the mid-point and should be a series of slow curves and angular movements, with an equal distribution of movements in the vertical and horizontal planes.

T6789 *Criterion Behaviour* — As in T2, T3, T4, T5, except that the child's eyes *and head* move in following the object.

Presentation — The presentation used to elicit T2 to T5 may be used to explore these responses. One procedural difference may be necessary. If the child does not move his head while following the object, the size of the movements should be increased so that they exceed the limits imposed by eye movements.

T10
(S1
person)
Criterion Behaviour — The child follows with eyes and head an object which is slowly pulled or is rolling slowly along a surface in front of him *or* a person moving across his visual field.

Presentation — The child's attention should be attracted to a pull-along toy or ball. Once he is looking at the toy it should be pulled or the ball rolled along a surface at a distance of about 40 cms in front of the child. Alternatively the child may follow a person who has attracted his attention and is moving across his visual field.

T11
(SS1)
Criterion Behaviour — The child will adjust his position in such a way that he can continue to see a slowly moving object which is going behind a screen.

Presentation — The child's attention is drawn to the object which he should visually fixate. The object is then slowly moved so that it passes behind the screen. The child should be given ample time to adjust his position to follow the object as it passes behind the screen. The position of the screen in relation to the child is of crucial importance. It should be sufficiently close to ensure that small movements of the child's head or body significantly increase the range of his vision.

T12
(SS8)
Criterion Behaviour — The child looks at an object and follows its movements along a trajectory which passes behind him. The child then turns his head to locate the object as it reappears. The child may show equivalent behaviour when an adult walks behind him.

Presentation — The object should be presented at the side of the child and his attention drawn to it. The object is then slowly moved behind the child to reappear on his other side. This behaviour may also be seen if examiner walks quietly across behind the child.

T13
(SS3)
Criterion Behaviour — The child's eyes initially follow an object moving rapidly in a horizontal or vertical plane, they lose the object because of its speed, but flick rapidly in the direction it was moving and successfully relocate it.

Presentation — The object is presented at the centre of the visual field at a distance of 40 cms. Once the child is looking at the object it is moved slowly in a vertical or horizontal direction to a point about 40 cms from the mid-point. Whilst the child is still looking at the object it is dropped in full view on to a soft pad or moved suddenly back across the child's visual field.

T14
(SS4)
Criterion Behaviour — The child's eyes initially follow an object which moves rapidly along an irregular trajectory. Because of its speed and eccentric motion the eyes lose their fixation upon it. The child looks for the object and locates it.

Presentation — The object is presented at the centre of the visual field at a distance of 40 cms. When the child is looking, the object should be moved in a series of curves and angular movements, with equal distribution of movements in vertical and horizontal planes stopping at a point on the edge of the visual field.

T15
(SS2)
Criterion Behaviour — The child will adjust his position in such a way that he is able to relocate an object which has slowly passed from sight behind a screen.

Presentation — As in T11 with the following modifications. Examiner should be certain that the screen and child are in such a relationship (bearing in mind any physical handicaps that the child may have) that the child can move to a position from which the stationary object can be seen. This item can be assessed at the same presentations as Item 11, by putting the object in a position which requires more physical movement than that involved in delaying the disappearance of the object.

T16
(SS5)
Criterion Behaviour — The child looks intently to or explores the position from which a slowly moving object *appeared* or at which it *disappeared*.

Presentation — Two screens are used. They are positioned about 20 cms apart. The object is moved across the gap between the screens and left behind the second screen.

T17
(SS6)
Criterion Behaviour — The child visually follows an object through a falling trajectory until it disappears behind a screen. The child then moves to rediscover the object.

Presentation — The object should be dropped onto a soft pad which deadens the sound of falling. The screen should hide the point where the object falls. It is important that the child should be able to physically reach the screen and object without great effort.

T18
(SS9)
Criterion Behaviour — When an object which is moving horizontally passes out of sight behind a screen the child will shift his gaze to the point where the object would appear if it continued along its original path.

Presentation — The object is shown to the child about 20 cms to one side of the screen. When the child is looking, move the object slowly behind the screen. Care should be taken to avoid giving cues by arm movement.

T19
(E31)

Criterion Behaviour — The child throws an object, e.g. a ball and watches its flight and landing.

Presentation — The child may pick up and throw the ball or other objects spontaneously. If necessary he is encouraged to throw them.

4. VISUO-MOTOR

This section covers Finger Play, Grasping, Reach and Grasp, and Gross and Fine Visuo-Motor Integration.

Equipment

Ten 2 cms red cubes in box, six small toys, three toy cars, ball, stand 4x4x6 cms.

V1   *Criterion Behaviour* — The child plays with his fingers. Both hands may be placed in his mouth together. Bringing together of his hands and taking hands to his mouth is controlled. It is apparently not chance occurrence.

        Presentation — Observational item.

V2   *Criterion Behaviour* — The child appears to be interested by his own hand movements — he tries to follow their motion when they catch his visual attention. However, the hand movements do not appear to be visually regulated, the hands are likely to move from the visual field with the child apparently unable to retain visual contact.

        Presentation — Observational item.

V3   *Criterion Behaviour* — When the child is playing and his hand
(S6)   is grasped and restrained, he turns and looks at the point of restraint.

        Presentation — The child's hand should be grasped in such a way that he cannot continue playing.

V4   *Criterion Behaviour* — The child holds an object, e.g. a 2 cms red cube, for more than five seconds when it is placed in his hands or when he grasps it spontaneously.

        Presentation — The object should be placed in the child's hand and held until the fingers close, or until examiner is certain that grasping is unlikely to occur. This item may also be scored if the child is observed to grasp and retain an object for five seconds or more.

V5 *Criterion Behaviour* — When the child's hand chances to come into contact with an object it is grasped, BUT — the child does not look at the object or put it in his mouth.

Presentation — As in V4. Observe visual or oral exploration when objects are grasped.

V6 *Criterion Behaviour* — The child's hand will close when the palm is lightly touched.

Presentation — When the child is in a content awake state, the palm of his hand should be pressed lightly for a period of 10 seconds. Both hands should be assessed.

V7 *Criterion Behaviour* — The child holds an object for more than thirty seconds when it is placed in his hand, or when he grasps it spontaneously.

Presentation — As in V4.

V8 (E8) *Criterion Behaviour* — The child holds an object at or near his midline and manipulates it with both hands.

Presentation — The object is handed to the child or he is observed in spontaneous play.

V9 (E9) *Criterion Behaviour* — The child transfers an object from one hand to the other at least twice.

Presentation — As in V8.

V10 *Criterion Behaviour* — When a cube is placed in each of the child's hands, he grasps them and holds them both for at least *three* seconds.

Presentation — Examiner puts a cube into each of the child's hands and encourages him to hold them.

V11 *Criterion Behaviour* — When an object is presented close to the child's hand, and in the same visual field as the hand, the child will move his hand and grasp the object.

Presentation — The object should be presented in such a way that E is certain that the child has seen it. It should then be slowly moved, so that the child's eyes follow it, until it reaches a position near to the child's hand. Examiner should be certain that the child is looking at the object when it has reached this position. If the child does not grasp the object even on encouragement, another object should be presented using the same procedure. A range of objects should be used.

V12   *Criterion Behaviour* — The child tries and fails to grasp a cube on a flat surface. In this item the child is credited with the attempt to grasp an object.

Presentation —The cube is put within grasping range, the child's attention is drawn to it and he is encouraged to take it. *NB.* V12, V13 and V14 test simultaneously.

V13   *Criterion Behaviour* — The child reaches and grasps the cube successfully with one hand or both hands.

Presentation — As in V12.

V14   *Criterion Behaviour* — When a cube is placed before the child at a readily accessible point, his attention is drawn to it and he is encouraged to obtain it, he reaches and deftly grasps it with one hand.

Presentation — As in V12.

V15   *Criterion Behaviour* — When the child reaches for and grasps an object which is not presented in the same visual field as his hand.

Presentation — The child's attention should be drawn to an object which at the moment of presentation is not in the same visual field as the child's hands. For example, when the child's hands are in his lap the object should be put upon the table and the child encouraged to get it. If grasping does not occur, a second object should be shown using the same procedure. Alternatively the object is held in a position away from the child's hand and he is encouraged to get it.

V16   *Criterion Behaviour* — The child shows evidence of being able to distinguish between the objects within grasping range, and those beyond this range.

Presentation — Objects known to be of interest to the child are placed within and beyond grasping range. If the child moves forward or points at objects beyond grasping range, or if he refuses to reach for objects beyond his range after having picked them up when nearer he is credited.

V17 *Criterion Behaviour* — The child moves to obtain an object placed beyond his reach.

Presentation — An object which is known to be interesting to the child is placed 4 cms beyond his most extended reach in such a position that by moving bodily he can obtain it. He should be encouraged to obtain the object.

V18 *Criterion Behaviour* — The child is able to distinguish between
(P14) an object which he wants and a small support. He grasps the object directly, ignoring the support.

Presentation — A small consumable object is placed upon a support e.g. a block (about 4x4x6 cms). The child is then encouraged to obtain the object.

V19 *Criterion Behaviour* — When the child grasps an object, he examines it visually.

Presentation — The object may be put in the child's hand or he may pick up objects spontaneously during the assessment.

V20 *Criterion Behaviour* — The child rotates the object with one
(E4) hand or both hands whilst looking at it. He appears to be interested in looking at all parts of the object.

Presentation — The object may be placed in the child's hand or picked up spontaneously.

5. AUDITORY

This section covers basic responsiveness to sound, audio-visual integration, response to the human voice and noise production in play.

Equipment
Chime bells, small handbell, rattle, six small toys including three squeaky toys which can be operated very easily, 4.5 cms wooden cubes.

Test items

A1 *Criterion Behaviour* — The child's eyes blink and/or his limbs are rapidly jerked in response to an unexpected sound.

Presentation — To avoid distressing the child the softest sounds should be presented first and louder sound only used when no response is shown. Sounds within the range of a loud whisper are defined as being soft; within the range of shouting as loud. Sounds should be produced at the side of the child outside his visual field, in this way they are likely to be both unexpected and inclined to produce head turning. It is suggested that the child should be attending to some quiet toy presented, or being manipulated, at his mid-line.
   Careful note should be made of both the nature and the intensity of the sound. Sounds should include the human voice of varied pitch and timbre.

A2 *Criterion Behaviour* — The child cries or smiles in response to sounds.

Presentation — As in A1. These changes in state should be noted when A1 is administered.

A3 *Criterion Behaviour* — The child reliably turns his eyes in the direction of a sound produced at the side of his head.

Presentation — As in A1. Presentation should be randomized. Three successive clear movements of the eyes in the correct direction scores on this item.

A4   *Criterion Behaviour* — The child reliably turns both his head and eyes in the direction of a sound produced at the side of his head.

         Presentation — As in A3.

A5   *Criterion Behaviour* — The child selectively responds to his
(S3)   name by turning, face brightening, ceasing activity, etc.

         Presentation — This item may be formally examined by calling the child's name when he is involved in some task. One method of establishing whether or not the child discriminates *his* name is to call other names or words the child is unlikely to be familiar with before calling his name. This item may also be scored if at any time during the assessment the child gives a clear indication that he knows his name.

A6   *Criterion Behaviour* — The child attends to a familiar nursery
(S4)   rhyme spoken to him by examiner. The child should cease other activities, look at examiner, and watch him with an attentive expression.

         Presentation — Examiner should be sure that the child is attending and then recite 'Humpty Dumpty', 'Three Blind Mice', etc., clearly but *without* added mime or other movements.

A7   *Criterion Behaviour* — The child pats or hits a squeaky toy so
(E17)   that it produces a sound at least three times.

         Presentation — A squeaky toy is given to the child who is allowed to play with it. If the child does not hit or pat the toy, the examiner should demonstrate and prompt. Record whether demonstration or prompting is necessary to elicit the response.

A8   *Criterion Behaviour* — The child hits a surface with one or
(E19)   both hands.

         Presentation — Behaviour may be observed when the child is at a table or on the floor. Examiner should record whether hitting is gentle or vigorous.

A9   *Criterion Behaviour* — The child hits an object with one or
(E18)   both hands.

Presentation — A rattle or squeaky toy should be placed on a
surface near the child or suspended within reach.

A10   *Criterion Behaviour* — The child makes deliberate appro-
(E21)   priate movements with an object which creates varied noises.
As the child plays he 'listens', and changes intensity or
direction of movements, etc.

Presentation — The rattle is given to the child.

A11   *Criterion Behaviour* — The child squeezes a squeaky toy so
(E22)   that it produces a sound. At least three noise-producing
responses are necessary to score on this item.

Presentation — A squeaky toy is given to the child who is
allowed to play with it. If the child does not squeeze the toy,
examiner should demonstrate the noise. Record whether
demonstration or prompting is necessary.

Auditory — Interview

AR1   Does he respond to any sound?
Probe for examples.

AR2   Does he respond to sounds within the volume range of normal speech?
By turning, smiling, startling etc.
Probe: What sounds? What does he do?

AR3   Does he respond correctly to his name?
If yes, how does he respond?
Probe:
By answering
Coming to you
Turning
Smiling
Repeating name
Will he do this with anyone?

AR4   Does he respond consistently to any sound?
Probe:
Like nursery rhymes
Goes to the door on hearing a knock
Laughs at particular sounds
Claps to tunes or music
Please state your example.

AR5   Does he hit or bang things when he is playing?
Probe for examples.

6. POSTURAL CONTROL

This section consists of interview items. The interview can be completed with the parent or teacher or may be used as a checklist to be filled in when the examiner is thoroughly familiar with the child.

Control of head

PC1   Which statements are the nearest to correct?

(a) When sitting, or held in the upright position, he can hold his head up and turn it either way with full control.

(b) When sitting, or held in the upright position, he can hold his head up for a short time — 5 seconds or more.

(c) When lying down he is able to turn his head from side to side.

(d) When lying down he is unable to turn his head.

(e) What methods are used to assist the child's head control? Please describe.

Sitting

PC2   Which statements are the nearest to correct?

(a) Can sit *firmly and safely* on a 'dining room' chair and eat food or play in this position.

(b) Can sit on a 'dining room' chair, but he cannot be left as he might tumble over.

(c) Can sit *firmly and safely* on the floor and can eat or play safely in this position.

(d) Can sit on the floor, but it is necessary to place cushions around him or be close at hand as he might tumble over.

(e) Needs support to enable him to sit.

If the final statement in the above list is true please describe what sort of support is necessary in PC3.

(f) All his weight has to be taken by an adult holding him or by harness; he hasn't the *strength* or necessary *muscular control* to sit without such help.

(g) Needs to be propped up by cushions, or strapped, or held, to stop him falling over — as yet he is *unable* to balance.

PC3   The usual support is:
    (a) Wheel chair with straps
    (b) Wheel chair with table
    (c) Baby chair with straps
    (d) Baby chair with table
    (e) Cushions
    (f) Other — please specify.

Standing

PC4   Which statements are the nearest to correct?
    (a) Can stand firmly *without* support.
    (b) Can stand *without* support — but is rather unsteady.
    (c) Can stand only *with* support — holds on to furniture, leans against walls, etc.
    (d) Can stand with the help of a standing board.
    (e) Can stand only with the support of an adult — he takes his weight.
    (f) Can stand only if the adult balances him and takes some of his weight.
    (g) Is unable to stand however supported.

7. EXPLORATORY PLAY

This section covers Oral Exploration, Visual Examination, Visuo-Motor Integration, Rolling, Pulling, Audio-Visuo-Motor Play, Throwing and Dropping.

Equipment

Six small toys, silent pull-along toy, ball, chime bars, small hand bell, rattle, plastic nut and bolt, screw barrels, spectacle case, three toy cars, dowels and peg board, tambourine, 4.5 cms wooden cubes, tin foil, newspaper, sandpaper boards, ring or toy on string.

Test items

E1   *Criterion Behaviour* — The child holds an object and places it against his mouth.

Presentation — The object is handed to the child or he is observed in free play.

E2   *Criterion Behaviour* — The child places an object against his mouth, where he licks, sucks or chews it.

Presentation — As in E1.

E3   *Criterion Behaviour* — The child visually examines an object which he had picked up.

Presentation — The object is handed to the child or he is observed in free play.

E4   *Criterion Behaviour* — The child rotates the object with one or
(V20)   both hands whilst looking at it. He appears to be interested in looking at all parts of the object.

Presentation — As in E1.

E5   *Criterion Behaviour* — The child deliberately removes pegs from their holes in a peg board.

Presentation — The child is given a board with a series of pegs loosely inserted in it — a board with six half inch by two inch dowels inserted loosely is ideal.

E6   *Criterion Behaviour* — The child fingers and visually examines component parts of an object. E.g. He will turn over a small bell and finger and visually inspect the clapper.

       Presentation — As in E1, with e.g. a small bell.

E7   *Criterion Behaviour* — When the child is sitting at a table, or where a solid edge or a surface is readily to hand, the child manipulates the edge with his fingers.

       Presentation — This behaviour may be observed when the child is sitting at a table or on the floor.

E8   *Criterion Behaviour* — The child holds an object at or near
(V8)   his mid-line and manipulates it with both hands.

       Presentation — As in E1.

E9   *Criterion Behaviour* — The child transfers an object from one hand to the other at least twice.

       Presentation — As in E1.

E10   *Criterion Behaviour* — The child separates two objects by unscrewing them.

       Presentation — The child is given an unscrewing toy — a large nut and bolt, unscrewing barrels, etc. — and is encouraged to unscrew them. If the child does not display the behaviour spontaneously examiner may demonstrate. Examiner should record whether the behaviour occurred spontaneously or after demonstration.

E11   *Criterion Behaviour* — The child uses his hands in a complementary manner which appears to be visually directed. The child watches his own movements and the results produced, unsuccessful responses being modified by visual feedback.

       Presentation — Virtually any object which evokes a coordinated two-handed behaviour may be used. Suggested objects are a spectacle case with a weak spring into which is placed a 'desired' object; nesting barrels which require unscrewing; a spring lidded box where one hand is required to prevent the lid closing while the other hand explores the contents. Examiner may demonstrate, record if prompting or demonstration is needed.

E12   *Criterion Behaviour* — The child pushes an object along a surface. The object may be a car, a brick or other object. Deliberate pushing which will usually be watched or done for its own sake and should not be confused with pushing or sweeping objects aside. *N.B.* cars etc. need not be correct way up with wheels on surface. They are objects to be pushed and the representational element involved in using them in a 'car like' fashion is covered in item E9.

       Presentation — As in E1.

E13   *Criterion Behaviour* — The child pushes a car along with its wheels on the surface of the table or floor. The car is held the correct way up while it is being pushed along.

       Presentation — A small car should be presented upside down to the child. Thus the child must turn the car the correct way up to score on this item.

E14   *Criterion Behaviour* — The child takes an object and rolls it along a convenient surface. This may be flat or sloping where the child positions the object so that it rolls down the slope.

       Presentation — Where possible, a sloping surface should be provided among the items available for the child to play with; together with a ball, toy car, etc.

E15   *Criterion Behaviour* — The child pulls the object toward himself or along the floor.

       Presentation — As in E1, with a small pull-along car.

E16   *Criterion Behaviour* — The child plays at rolling a ball when he
(CP4) is playing on his own. He throws or pushes it along the floor, moves after it and repeats the response. Alternatively he may roll the ball from hand to hand or against the wall. This activity to be completed at least twice to score.

       Presentation — As in E1.

E17
(A7)
Criterion Behaviour — The child pats or hits a squeaky toy so that it produces a sound at least three times.

Presentation — A squeaky toy is given to the child who is allowed to play with it. If the child does not pat or hit the toy, examiner should demonstrate and prompt. Record whether demonstration or prompting is necessary to elicit a response.

E18
(A9)
Criterion Behaviour — The child hits an object with one or both hands.

Presentation — A rattle should be placed on a surface near the child or suspended within reach.

E19
(A8)
Criterion Behaviour — When playing on his own, the child hits a surface with one or both hands.

Presentation — Behaviour observed when the child is at a table or sitting on the floor. Examiner should record whether hitting is gentle or vigorous.

E20
Criterion Behaviour — The child shakes an object — simple shaking with little apparent attention or variation in the activity.

Presentation — As in E1. A non-sound-producing object should be used.

E21
(A10)
Criterion Behaviour — The child makes deliberate appropriate movements with an object which creates varied noises. As the child plays he 'listens', and changes intensity and direction of movements etc.

Presentation — The rattle is given to the child.

E22
(A11)
Criterion Behaviour — The child squeezes a squeaky toy so that it produces a sound: At least three noise producing responses are necessary to score on this item.

Presentation — A squeaky toy is given to the child who is allowed to play with it. If the child does not squeeze the toy, examiner should demonstrate the noise. Record whether demonstration or prompting is necessary.

E23   *Criterion Behaviour* — The child takes an object and repeatedly
(A12)   hits or taps it against a nearby surface. There is no apparent
        deliberate variation in the manner of the hitting or the surface
        used.

        Presentation — The object, e.g. a cube or the rattle, may be
        picked up by the child or put in his hand whilst he sits at the
        table.

E24   *Criterion Behaviour* — The child deliberately knocks down
        towers of cubes made by himself or by the examiner.

        Presentation — A tower of four or five bricks is built by the ex-
        aminer, the child is encouraged to knock them down, if
        necessary by demonstration.

E25   *Criterion Behaviour* — The child hits an object in a varied way
        whilst 'concentrating' on the different effects produced.
        Examiner should look for variation in the heaviness/speed of
        the blows or different surfaces being struck.

        Presentation — The child is given a stick, tambourine and
        chime bells. If necessary he is prompted to hit the objects.

E26   *Criterion Behaviour* — The child crumples tin foil or newspaper
        with one or both hands.

        Presentation — The newspaper or tin foil should make a noise
        when crumpled. Examiner may observe the child or prompt
        and demonstrate.

E27   *Criterion Behaviour* — The child touches or rubs an object
        against a rough surface.

        Presentation — As in E1. Sandpaper boards or other rough
        surfaces should be available.

E28   *Criterion Behaviour* — When playing on his own or when given
(A13)   two objects, the child holds one object in each hand and
        bangs them together at least three times.

        Presentation — An object is placed in each of the child's hands,
        or two objects are picked up by the child.

E29   *Criterion Behaviour* — The child throws objects but appears to
        have little or no interest in the trajectory and landing of the
        object, it is the act of throwing itself which is all important.

        Presentation — As in E1.

E30   *Criterion Behaviour* — The child drops an object and watches
        the act of *releasing*, but he appears to have little or no interest in
        the falling object — he concentrates on the act of releasing the
        object.

        Presentation — As in E1.

E31   *Criterion Behaviour* — The child throws an object, e.g. a ball,
(T19)   and watches its flight and landing.

        Presentation — As in E 1. If necessary the child is encouraged
        to throw objects.

E32   *Criterion Behaviour* — The child dangles and swings an object
        by the string attached to it and watches the object swinging.

        Presentation — A ring attached to a string or a small toy with
        a string attached is given to the child. Examiner should
        prompt and demonstrate if the behaviour does not occur
        spontaneously. If prompts or demonstrations are used they
        should be recorded.

E33   *Criterion Behaviour* — The child drops the object, retrieves it
        and drops it again. The trajectory of the falling object is
        watched as is its landing. The child varies the position from
        which the object is dropped. It is its fall and the manner in
        which it lands which appears to hold the child's attention and
        stimulate him to vary the dropping.

        Presentation — As in E1 with a ball or other object.

8. CONSTRUCTIVE PLAY

This section deals with selected aspects of constructive play with a ball, drawing and play with cubes. Representational and symbolic play is not explicitly assessed.

Equipment

Sheets of paper, nylon or felt tip pens or crayon, ball, 4.5 cms cubes, wastepaper basket, stacking toy with blind ring.

Test items

CP1   *Criterion Behaviour* — The child can throw a ball. Throwing is defined as releasing the ball after a definite movement of the arm, the ball moving in approximately the direction the child is facing.

        Presentation — Examiner gives the ball to the child, and initially watches his free play. If throwing does not take place before the ball is discarded, examiner should return the ball to the child and encourage him verbally and by gesture to throw the ball. If the above strategy fails, examiner should demonstrate throwing and encourage the child to imitate. Record demonstration if this is a necessary strategy.

CP2   *Criterion Behaviour* — The child has sufficient control over his throwing to deliberately hit a target.

        Presentation — A large wastepaper basket with an opening about 30 cms across should be placed about 60 cms, in front of the child. He should be encouraged verbally, by gesture and by demonstration t throw the ball into the basket.

CP3   *Criterion Behaviour* — The child plays at rolling a ball with
(S10)   examiner. The child throws the ball along the floor or pushes it in the direction of the experimenter who sends it back. The child should roll the ball back at least twice to score.

        Presentation — Examiner takes up a position facing the child, either across a table or on the floor, he rolls the ball to the child and encourages him to roll it back.

CP4
(E16)
Criterion Behaviour — The child plays at rolling the ball by himself. He throws or pushes it along the floor, moves after it and repeats the response. Alternatively he may roll the ball from hand to hand or against the wall. This activity should be completed at least twice to score.

Presentation — The child should be given a ball about 5 cms in diameter and observe in free play.

CP5
Criterion Behaviour — The child makes some attempt to mark paper with a felt tip, or nylon tipped pen or crayon without any demonstration. To score the pen or crayon must come in contact with the paper although the child does not necessarily mark the paper to score.

Presentation — The child is given a crayon, felt or nylon tipped pen, and allowed to mark a large sheet of paper fixed in front of him.

CP6
Criterion Behaviour — The child produces spontaneous *line* scribbling. The strokes are approximately straight lines on the paper in any direction. Each stroke need not be a discrete movement, a 'zig-zag' or approximately straight lines score.

Presentation — As in CP5.

CP7
Criterion Behaviour — The child makes definite strokes on the paper, which are approximately straight. Instead of the pencil being 'zig-zagged' across the paper the pencil is lifted from the paper on completion of each line.

Presentation — As in CP5.

CP8
Criterion Behaviour — The child produces spontaneous *circular* scribbling. The general movement of the child's hand is circular, although the resulting scribble may appear like a ragged, intermittent series of overlapping loops.

Presentation — As in CP5.

CP9
Criterion Behaviour — The child spontaneously produces approximations to circles. Instead of the pencil being 'stirred' on the

surface of the paper as in the circular scribbling, the pencil will tend to be lifted from the paper on completion of a circle.

Presentation — As in CP5.

CP10
(I15)
Criterion Behaviour — When the examiner draws and scribbles on a piece of paper which is placed directly in front of the child at a distance of about 40 cms, the child watches for at least one second.

Presentation — A sheet of white paper and a pencil, felt or nylon tipped pen is used. The child is encouraged to watch.

CP11
Criterion Behaviour — The child will make some attempt to imitate examiner's scribbling — some marks will be made on the paper.

Presentation — The child — after he has watched the examiner drawing — should be encouraged to use the pen or crayon verbally and by 'interesting' demonstration, e.g. examiner scribbling vigorously.

CP12
(I15)
Criterion Behaviour — When the examiner draws and scribbles on a piece of paper which is placed directly in front of the child at a distance of about 40 cms., the child watched for about ten seconds plus.

Presentation — As in CP10.

CP13
Criterion Behaviour — The child successfully produces scribbled lines, circles, discrete lines or directional strokes in imitation of examiner.

Presentation — Examiner should get the child's attention and demonstrate the various models. He should hand the pencil to the child and encourage him to perform in the same way, prompting and rewarding as necessary.

CP14
Criterion Behaviour — When playing with a ring stacking toy, the child discriminated a round block with no hole from rings similar in all other aspects, and does *not* attempt to place it over the stacking peg. Other responses should be noted.

Presentation — The round blocks should be similar in all respects to the other rings used except for the absence of the hole. This is most easily done where a wooden toy is used and the block is made to match those supplied.

CP15 *Criterion Behaviour* — The child builds a tower with cubes. This may occur spontaneously, in imitation of examiner or after verbal instruction, prompting and demonstration.

Presentation — Eight cubes should be put within easy reach of the child and he should be allowed to play with them. If the child does not build a tower spontaneously, examiner should encourage him to build by prompting, demonstrations or verbal encouragement and reward.

CP16 *Criterion Behaviour* — The child makes, and pushes for a distance of at least 10 cms, a 'train' of no less than three cubes, spontaneously or in imitation of examiner.

Presentation — Examiner attracts the child's attention by calling his name, tapping a cube on the table, etc. He then says '. . . do this' and places four cubes in a line on the table. He then pushes the line to and fro across the table top making a noise like an old-fashioned trainhooter. Examiner then says '. . . do it, you make train'. If the child succeeds in making the train and pushes it the required distance, he should be warmly reinforced. Note whether the child also imitates the sound made by examiner.

CP17 *Criterion Behaviour* — The child builds a bridge with three cubes spontaneously or imitation of examiner.

Presentation — Examiner takes all but three cubes from the child, he retains three for himself and puts the remainder away. Examiner attracts the child's attention by calling his name, tapping a cube on the table, etc., he then says '. . . do this', and places two cubes close to each other and bridges the gap with a third cube. If the child succeeds in building a similar structure, he should be warmly reinforced.

C18 *Criterion Behaviour* — The child, when given free access to cubes, spontaneously arranges them in patterns on the table top. He may form squares, 'regiments', etc.

Presentation — The child is given ten wooden cubes and his free play scored on the relevant criteria.

CP19   *Criterion Behaviour* — The child, when given free access to cubes, spontaneously builds structures more complex than a simple tower, train or bridge.

Presentation — As in C18.

CP20   *Criterion Behaviour* — When allowed free play with cubes the child 'experiments' with their balancing properties. He may gently push a cube to the edge of another until it just balances, build an 'erratic' tower placing additional bricks to compensate for the lean, gently push a tower to the virtual point of toppling then let it rock back, etc.

Presentation — As in C18.

9. SEARCH STRATEGIES

This section covers items concerned with the attainment of the object concept and its elaboration in search strategies. They cover Following, Prediction of Movement, Simple and Complex Search, and Search in Play.

Equipment

Six small toys, three toy cars, selection of sweets, two opaque screens, soft pad, stand 4x4x6 cms, three dome-shaped hollow covers each 10 cms in diameter made of rubber balls cut in half. All should be the same size, colour and texture. Orange-coloured cloth approximately 30x30 cms, 60 cms of cord, a rake, three boxes about 10x10 cms.

Test items

SS1
(T11)
Criterion Behaviour — The child will adjust his position in such a way that he can continue to see a slowly moving object which is going behind a screen.

Presentation — The child's attention is drawn to the object which he should visually fixate. The object is then slowly moved so that it passes behind the screen. The child should be given ample time to adjust his position to follow the object as it passes behind the screen. The position of the screen in relation to the child is of crucial importance. It should be sufficiently close to ensure that small movements of the child's head or body significantly increase the range of his vision.

SS2
(T15)
Criterion Behaviour — The child will adjust his position in such a way that he is able to relocate an object which has slowly passed from sight behind a screen.

Presentation — As in item S1 with the following modifications. Examiner should be certain that the screen and child are in such a relationship (bearing in mind any physical handicaps that the child may have) that the child can move to a position from which the stationary object can be visually relocated. This item can be assessed at the same time as the presentation of item

SS1 by finally putting the object in a position which requires more physical movement than that involved in delaying the disappearance of the object.

SS3
(T13)
Criterion Behaviour — The child's eyes initially follow an object moving rapidly in a horizontal or vertical plane, the eyes lose the object because of its speed but flick rapidly in the direction it was moving and successfully relocate it.

Presentation — The object is presented at the centre of the visual field at a distance of 40 cms. Once the child is looking at the object, it is moved slowly in a horizonal or vertical plane to a point about 40 cms from the mid-point. When the child is still looking at the object it is dropped on to a soft pad or moved suddenly back across the child's visual field.

SS4
(T14)
Criterion Behaviour — The child's eyes initally follow an object which moves rapidly along an irregular trajectory. Because of its speed and eccentric motion the eyes lose their fixation on it. The child then looks for the object and locates it.

Presentation — The object is presented in the centre of the visual field at a distance of 40 cms. When the child is looking, the object should be moved in a series of curves and angular movements, with equal distribution of movements in the vertical and horizontal planes, stopping at a point on the edge of the visual field.

SS5
(T16)
Criterion Behaviour — The child explores or looks intently at the position from which a slowly moving object appeared or at which it disappeared.

Presentation — Two screens are used. They are positioned about 20 cms apart. The object is moved across the gap between the screens and left behind the second screen.

SS6
(T17)
Criterion Behaviour — The child visually follows an object through a falling trajectory until it disappears behind a screen. The child then moves to rediscover the object.

Presentation — The object should be dropped on to a soft pad. The screen should hide the point where the object falls.

SS7   *Criterion Behaviour* — When the child has seen an object hidden under two screens he still searches for and obtains the object.

Presentation — The object is put under a half ball cover. A second screen, an orange cloth, is then laid over the ball. The child is not allowed to begin searching for the object for three seconds following the completion of the procedure.

SS8
(T12)   *Criterion Behaviour* — The child looks at an object and follows its movements along a trajectory which passes behind him. The child then turns his head to relocate the object as it reappears.

Presentation — The object should be presented at the side of the child and his attention drawn to it. The object is slowly moved behind the child to reappear to him on his other side. This behaviour may also be seen if examiner walks quietly behind the child.

SS9
(T18)   *Criterion Behaviour* — When an object which is moving horizontally passes out of sight behind a screen, the child will shift his gaze to the point where the object would appear if it continued along its original path.

Presentation — The object is shown to the child about 20 cms to one side of the screen. When the child is looking move the object slowly behind the screen. Care should be taken to avoid giving cues by arm movements.

SS10
(P4)   *Criterion Behaviour* — When an object is partially hidden beneath a screen within easy grasping distance of the child, the child obtains the object.

Presentation — The object is put on the table and the child's attention drawn to it. The half ball is then put over the object so that it partially covers it. A delay of about three seconds is imposed between the completion of the presentation procedure and encouraging or allowing the child to respond.

SS11   *Criterion Behaviour* — The child unwraps a cloth that was folded round an object whilst he was watching. He ignores the cloth once it has been removed.

Presentation — An object is issued that has been found to be rewarding for the child e.g. a sweet wrapped in a plain cloth. The child is encouraged to get the object by unwrapping it.

SS12   *Criterion Behaviour* — When an object is *seen clearly* by the child to be put under a screen within easy grasping distance, he removes and obtains the object.

Presentation — The object is shown to the child and is held so that it is fully visible until it is covered by the half ball. A delay of about three seconds should be imposed between covering the object and encouraging or allowing the child to get it.

SS13   *Criterion Behaviour* — When an object is *clearly seen* by the child to be placed beneath one of *two* screens, both within easy grasping distance, the child correctly locates the object on three consecutive trials. The hiding position is randomized.

Presentation — The object is shown to the child and is held so that it is fully visible until it is covered by the half ball. The hiding position is randomized. A delay of about three seconds is imposed between covering the object and encouraging or allowing the child to get it.

SS14   *Criterion Behaviour* — When an object is *clearly seen* by the child to be placed beneath one of *three* screens all within easy grasping distance, the child correctly locates the object on three consecutive trials. The cover under which the object is hidden is randomized in relation to position.

Presentation — All three half-ball covers are used. The object is shown to the child and is held so that it is fully visible until it is covered by the half ball. The hiding position is randomized. A delay of about three seconds is used as before.

SS15   *Criterion Behaviour* — When an object is hidden in examiner's hand and his hand moves beneath one of two covers where the object is left, the empty hand being shown to the child, the child correctly locates the object on three consecutive trials. The hiding position is randomized.

Presentation — The procedure is identical to that used in S12, with the following exception. The object is *totally concealed* within the examiner's hand, it is *not seen* during the act of hiding. The child should clearly see the object going into e's hand and should be very clearly shown the empty hand once the object has been hidden. A delay of about three seconds is imposed as before.

SS16   *Criterion Behaviour* — When an object is hidden within examiner's hand and his hand moves beneath one of three covers where the object is deposited and the empty hand is then shown to the child, the child correctly locates the object on three consecutive trials. The hiding position is randomized.

     Presentation — The procedure is identical to that used in S14 with the exception that three screens are used.

SS17   *Criterion Behaviour* — When an object is concealed within hand and the hand is passed beneath each of three covers in turn, the object being left under one of them, and the child having no indication under which cover the object has been left, he will search under the covers until he locates the object.

     Presentation — The object is shown to the child and is then totally concealed within e's hand so that it is not seen while passing beneath the three covers nor when it is hidden. A small sweet or other preferred object should be used. Each cover should be lifted in turn, no cue being given as to the position when the object is left. Once the hand has come from under the last cover it should be shown to be empty to the child. Examiner should be certain that the child has attended to the entire sequence. The hiding procedure should be randomized with respect to sequence of covers lifted and position at which object is left. A delay of about three seconds should be imposed between the completion of the presentation procedure and encouraging or allowing the child to respond.

SS18   *Criterion Behaviour* — When an object is hidden in examiner's hand and the hand is passed beneath each of three covers in turn, *but* the object is not placed under any of them, examiner retaining it in his hand, the child will search under the covers then turn his attention to e's hand where he will find the object.

Presentation — Exactly as in SS17 except the examiner retains the object in his hand. The hand containing the object should be positioned within easy reach of the child immediately it appears from beneath the final screen.

SS19   *Criterion Behaviour* — The child takes the lids from simple, easily opened boxes. Removing the lids should appear to be a deliberate act, i.e. if the lid comes off when the box is shaken or thrown the item should not be credited.

Presentation — The child is given a number of boxes with simple lids. The lids should be of a simple lift-off type.

SS20   *Criterion Behaviour* — The child searches or asks in some way, for an object that is not present. It is not the *disappearance* of the object which starts the search but rather noting that the object is absent.

Presentation — A favoured toy that the child brings to the assessment session serves well. Alternatively use an object which the child develops a liking for in the sessions. The object should be hidden while the child is involved in another activity. If at any point during the assessment, or when the child is on the point of leaving, he looks for the toy without prompting, the item should be credited.

SS21   *Criterion Behaviour* — The child hides and searches for objects in play.

Presentation — A number of objects some of which are capable of being concealed by the others, e.g. small toys and boxes, should be presented to the child and his free activity with them observed.

10. PERCEPTUAL PROBLEM SOLVING

This section deals with Negotiation of Screens, Cause and Effect and Complex Strategies for Handling Objects.

Equipment
2 cms cubes in box, six small toys, three toy cars, selection of sweets, two opaque screens, transparent screen, stand 4x4x6 cms, three half ball covers, orange cloth, 600 cms cord, rake, suction cup, rattling stick, string of beads, narrow necked container.

Test items

P1　*Criterion Behaviour* — When an obstacle is positioned between the child and a preferred object in such a way that the object remains visible but the obstacle impedes the child's efforts to obtain it, the child will knock down the obstacle and get the object.

　　Presentation — The screen should be light enough to be easily knocked down by the child. It should be put within striking distance and the object placed in a visible position just beyond it.

P2　*Criterion Behaviour* — When an obstacle is placed between the child and an object in such a way that the object remains visible but the obstacle impedes the child's efforts to obtain it, the child pulls or pushes or picks it up and moves it aside. He picks up the object.

　　Presentation — As in P1.

P3　*Criterion Behaviour* — When an obstacle is placed between the child and an object in such a way that the object remains visible but the child's efforts to obtain it are impeded, the child will reach round or over, or attempt to reach round or over, the obstacle. He picks up the object.

　　Presentation — As in P1.

P4　*Criterion Behaviour* — When an object is partially hidden beneath a screen within easy grasping distance of the child, the child gets the object.

Presentation — The object is put on the table and the child's attention drawn to it. The half ball is then put over the object so that it partially covers it. A delay of about three seconds is imposed between the completion of the presentation procedure and encouraging or allowing the child to respond to avoid the use of reaching response initiated before the object is correctly concealed.

P5   *Criterion Behaviour* — When an object is clearly seen by the child to be placed beneath a transparent screen within easy grasping distance of the child, he removes the screen and obtains the object.

Presentation — The object is shown to the child and is held so that it is fully visible as it is covered by transparent screen. A delay of about three seconds should be imposed between the completion of the presentation procedure and encouraging or allowing the child to respond.

P6   *Criterion Behaviour* — When an object is placed within the child's grasping range and a transparent screen is placed between the child and the object, the child will get the object by pushing the screen aside.

Presentation — As in P6 except that the child cannot see the object when the screen is in place. The screen should be positioned before the child has started reaching. A three second delay is imposed between positioning the screen and allowing the child to attempt to secure the object.

P7   *Criterion Behaviour* — When the child has watched a piece of cord being attached to an object, and the object is placed beyond his reach with the other end of the cord within easy grasping range, the child gets the object by pulling in the cord.

Presentation — The child should be very clearly shown that the object is being attached to the cord, it is then placed beyond the child's reach with the free end of the cord within easy grasping range. The object is positioned at the mid-line, with the cord lying at an angle of forty-five degrees to the child. The child thus has to reach *away* from the object to pick up the cord and is thus less likely to pull in the object 'accidentally'. The child should be encouraged to get the object, prompts should be used if necessary, and their use recorded.

P8   *Criterion Behaviour* — When an object is placed on a flat surface beyond the grasping distance of the child and a piece of cord is put beside it or over it, the child:

(a) pulls a little at the other end of the cord which is within easy grasping distance 'in experimentation' but does not continue with this behaviour;
(b) searches for an alternative means of obtaining the object, e.g. takes cord and attempts to lasso the object;
(c) looks at the object but does not do anything (thus indicating that he clearly discriminated when the cord can be used as a means of receiving the object and when it can not).

Presentation — As for P7 but the object is placed to the *side* of the cord, or positioned *above* it.

P9   *Criterion Behaviour* — When an object has been placed upon a readily movable support one side of which is within easy grasping range of the child, he will get the object by pulling the support towards himself.

Presentation — The piece of orange cloth can be used for the support. This is placed with its near edge within easy grasping range of the child, the far edge well beyond his reach. The object is then put on the cloth at a point beyond the grasping range of the child and he is encouraged to get it. This procedure should be tried a few times before prompts are given. These may be:

(a) Examiner gently pulls the support a few cms to demonstrate the functional relationship between the support and the object;
(b) pulls the cloth in and gets the object.

P10   *Criterion Behaviour* — When the child has watched a piece of cord being attached to an object which is then placed *below* the child with the other end of the cord within easy grasping distance, the child will draw up the cord and obtain the object.

Presentation — The child should be carefully shown that the object is being fixed on the cord. The object should then be placed in sight yet out of reach below the child. The free end of the cord should be placed within easy grasping range and the child encouraged to obtain it. Demonstrate and prompt if necessary.

P11   *Criterion Behaviour* — When an object is put beside or above a readily movable support at a point beyond grasping distance the child:

(a) pulls a little at the part of the support which is within easy grasping distance 'in experimentation' but does not continue with this behaviour.
(b) looks for an alternative way of getting the object;
(c) looks at the object but does not do anything.

Thus indicating that he clearly discriminates when the cord can be used as a means of obtaining the object and when it can not.
Allow about forty seconds to observe responses.

Presentation — As for P9 but the object is put to the side of the support or is positioned above.

P12   *Criterion Behaviour* — When an object has been grasped by the
(S5)   child but he is not able to manipulate it freely because examiner holds it, the child will try to push examiner's hand away.

Presentation — The object is put within easy grasping distance. Examiner holds on to the object while encouraging the child to get it and maintains his hold until the child either pushes his hand away or loses interest in the object.

P13   *Criterion Behaviour* — When the child is playing with an object
(S7)   and his play is restricted by one of his arms being grasped, the child attempts to push away the restraining hand.

Presentation — When the child is playing , the examiner should firmly grasp his arm and thus restrain him. The grasp should be continued until the child attempts to push the hand away, is distracted by an alternative activity, looks as if he might become upset, or one minute elapses.

P14
(V18)
Criterion Behaviour — The child is able to distinguish between the object he wants and a small support. He grasps the object directly, ignoring the support which is not grasped.

Presentation — A small object is placed upon a small support, e.g. a consumable object. The child is then encouraged to get the object.

P15
Criterion Behaviour — Under circumstances where the child's own body proves an impediment to his actions he will move his body appropriately.

Presentation — Sit the child on a colourful square of material during the assessment in such a way that the cloth protrudes at the side but is not immediately visible to the child. The item may be scored either when the child notices the cloth and tries to get it, or when it is pointed out to him and he is encouraged to get it. The child should be credited on this item if he shows any other behaviour which fits the criterion. The child may demonstrate this behaviour in a number of ways during the assessment, these should be noted and credited.

P16
Criterion Behaviour — The child removes contents from containers. He takes them out by hand or deliberately tips them out, i.e. by turning box on side rather than knocking box over.

Presentation — The child is given a container with small objects in it. The box containing small cubes is ideal.

P17
Criterion Behaviour — When an object is put beyond a child's reach above his head, and a stick or other suitable object is to hand, the child uses the stick to dislodge the object and get it.

Presentation — Any support which leaves the object visible and from which it can be easily dislodged is acceptable. It is suggested however that a rubber suction cup with a small perspex platform attached should be used. This has two advantages; it can be attached to a smooth surface at the height desired and the object is always fully visible.

The object should be placed upon the support positioned above and beyond the child's reach. A stick should have already been leant in a clearly visible position against the wall, table etc., below the object. If necessary the child is encouraged and prompted.

P18   *Criterion Behaviour* — A long stick is manipulated so that it readily passes between the uprights of a vertically barred obstacle.

Presentation — A colourful rattling stick (plastic pipe containing 'sleigh bells') is used as the object — other objects with similar shape qualities may be used. It is placed beyond a vertically barred barrier, purpose-built presentation box or cot. The object is left parallel with the front of the cot. If necessary the child is encouraged and prompted.

P19   *Criterion Behaviour* — The child uses a rake appropriately to obtain another object.

Presentation — The object should be placed beyond the child's grasping range. A small 'rake' is put on the table with its handle parallel to the edge. If necessary the child should be encouraged and prompted.

P20   *Criterion Behaviour* — When an object is placed above a child, beyond his reach, the child manages to bring himself within reach of the object by climbing on furniture etc., which he may move into position for that purpose.

Presentation — As for P17. The child may well ignore the stick, move furniture and climb upon it. If the stick is used correctly as in P17, it should be removed, the object should be placed elsewhere in the room beyond the child's reach and his behaviour observed for up to two minutes.

P21   *Criterion Behaviour* — The child puts a string of beads into a tall narrow container in one movement rather than 'bit by bit'. Two approaches are possible:

(a) to fold or roll up the beads and pop them in as a 'lump',
(b) to dangle the beads above the open top and lower them in.

Presentation — The beads are given to the child in the container which examiner should rattle in play. If the child does not tip them out spontaneously, examiner should do so. The child should then be encouraged to put them back so that they can be shaken and tipped out again.

P22   *Criterion Behaviour* — When a cube is offered to the free hand of a child who is already holding one cube, he takes the second cube with his free hand. To reach criterion he may retain both for three seconds or drop the first one.

       Presentation — The child is offered a cube. If he takes and holds it a second cube is offered.

P23   *Criterion Behaviour* — The child whilst holding one cube is shown a second. He should reach to grasp the second cube with his free hand even though he need not pick it up.

       Presentation — As in P21. If the child succeeds in grasping and holding the first cube then the second cube is put on the table.

P24   *Criterion Behaviour* — The child whilst holding one cube is shown second. He releases the first cube and picks up the second with his now empty preferred hand or picks up both cubes.

       Presentation — As in P21.

P25   *Criterion Behaviour* — The child on having grasped and held two cubes, one in each hand, is shown a third. He retains the two cubes already while looking at the third cube.

       Presentation — As in P21. Then, once the child has retained the two cubes for three seconds, the third cube is presented.

P26   *Criterion Behaviour* — The child, on having grasped and held two cubes, one in each hand, is presented with a third. While retaining the two cubes he tries to pick up the third cube.

       Presentation — As in P25.

P27   *Criterion Behaviour* — As P26 except that the child *succeeds* in picking up the block. His method should be recorded. He may either (a) Put two cubes into one hand — then grasping with free hand. (b) Use two hands, the third cube being held between them. (c) Use his mouth or chin. (d) Other effective means of picking up.

       Presentation — As in P25.

11. SOCIAL

This section covers test and interview components. The test items in the section cover basic responsiveness to adults in terms of Watching and Attending to Adult's voice, Awareness of Adult Restraint, Simple Cooperation and responses to his image in a Mirror. The interview component covers more general aspects of social responsiveness.

Equipment
Six small toys, three toy cars, picture book, ball, mirror.

Test items

S1
(T10)
Criterion Behaviour — The child's eyes follow a person moving across his visual field.

Presentation — Examiner should attract the child's attention by calling, waving, etc., and as soon as the child is looking he should slowly walk in front of the child watching his response.

S2
(I13)
Criterion Behaviour — The child inspects the examiner's face, looking from one feature to another.

Presentation — Examiner should position himself some 40 cms from the child's face in his direct line of vision whilst smiling and talking to the child.

S3
(AR3)
Criterion Behaviour — The child selectively responds to his name by turning face, brightening, ceasing activity, etc.

Presentation — This item may be formally examined by calling the child's name when he is involved in some task. One method of establishing whether or not the child discriminates his name is to call other names or words the child is unlikely to be familiar with, before calling his name. This item may also be scored if at any time during the assessment the child gives a clear indication that he discriminates his name.

S4
(AR5)
Criterion Behaviour — The child attends to familiar nursery rhyme spoken to him by examiner; the child should cease other

activities look at examiner and watch him with an 'alert' expression.

Presentation — Examiner should make sure that the child is attending and then recite 'Humpty Dumpty' or 'Hickory Dickory Dock', etc., clearly but without added mime or other movements.

S5
(P12)
Criterion Behaviour — When an object has been grasped by the child but he is not able to manipulate it freely because examiner holds it, the child will try to push examiner's hand away.

Presentation — The object is put within easy grasping distance. Examiner holds on to the object while encouraging the child to obtain it and maintains his hold until the child either pushes his hand away or loses interest in the object.

Alternatively, if the child makes no attempt to grasp the object while examiner holds it, he should wait until the child is playing with an object, then grasp the object and prevent the child from playing. Again grasp should be maintained until the child pushes his hand away or loses interest in the object.

When a small sweet is being used as the object, examiner should firmly place his index finger on the sweet while encouraging the child to obtain it.

S6
(V3)
Criterion Behaviour — When the child is playing and his hand is grasped and restrained he turns and looks at the point of restraint.

Presentation — The child's hand should be grasped in such a way that he cannot continue playing.

S7
(P13)
Criterion Behaviour — When the child is playing with an object and his play is restricted by one of his arms being grasped the child attempts to push away the restraining hand.

Presentation — When the child is playing, examiner should firmly grasp his arm and thus restrain him. The grasp should be continued until the child attempts to push the hand away, is distracted by an alternative activity, looks as if he might become upset, or one minute elapses.

S8   *Criterion Behaviour* — The child maintains his interest in
(I16)   looking at a book when an adult shows the pictures and talks to
          the child about them for at least *one minute*.

          Presentation — The child is given a sturdy book with simple
          coloured pictures. He is encouraged to look at the pictures.
          Keep trying for at least 30 seconds.

S9   *Criterion Behaviour* — The child treats a book appropriately,
(I16)   turns pages, points to pictures, smiles at pictures, babbles at
          pictures, names pictures etc.

          Presentation — As in S8.

S10   *Criterion Behaviour* — The child stops ongoing behaviour to
          attend to his reflection in a mirror.

          Presentation — When the child is at play, a mirror about 30 x
          28 cms is put directly in front of him at a distance of about
          40 cms. Examiner should be certain that it is possible for the
          child to see a clear reflection of himself.

S11   *Criterion Behaviour* — The child, on seeing his reflection in a
          mirror, moves towards it by leaning, stretching forward, sitting
          up, approaching, etc.

          Presentation — As in S10 except that examiner must make
          adjustments to the mirror that are necessary to maintain the
          child's reflection within his visual field as he approaches.

S12   *Criterion Behaviour* — The child fingers and pats his own
          reflection.

          Presentation — As in S10.

S13   *Criterion Behaviour* — The child smiles at his own reflection, his
          eyes concentrate on his reflected face.

          Presentation — As in S10.

S14   *Criterion Behaviour* — The child 'plays' with his mirror image.
          He laughs at it, pulls faces, waves, etc. He appears to be 'looking

for', or anticipating the changes that his own behaviour brings about in the reflection.

Presentation — As in S10.

S15 *Criterion Behaviour* — The child feels and looks behind the mirror, looks back to his reflection and looks behind again. He appears to be searching for the 'cause' or 'location' of the image.

Presentation — As in S10.

Interview

SR1 Does he play cooperatively with other children?
Probe: Examples.
NB Ensure that this is cooperation rather than parallel play.

SR2 Does he play cooperatively with adults?
Probe: Examples.

SR3 Does he request help from adults?
Probe: Examples.

SR4 Does he accept help from adults?
Probe: Examples.

SR5 Does he play with adults but insist on running the game so that you can't change the direction of what he is doing?
Probe: Examples.

SR6 Does he share toys with other children?
Probe: Examples.

SR7 Does he like other children?
Probe: Examples.

SR8 Does he show jealousy of other children?

SR9 Does he reject the approaches of other children?

SR10 Does he watch other children?

SR11   Does he usually do as he is told?
        Probe: Do you have to smack him or speak to him sharply very much?

SR12   How does he react when told 'no'?
        Probe: Does he show self-control?

12. COMMUNICATION

This section covers the understanding and use of a variety of forms of communication. It also allows assessment of the ability to imitate gross and fine motor responses and vocalization. The assessment involves several separate components:

I.	Communication Interview — Receptive Abilities
II.	Communication Interview — Development of sounds and imitation
III.	Communication Interview — Expressive Abilities
IV.	Expressive Vocabulary Test
V.	Receptive Vocabulary Test
VI.	Motor Imitation Test
VII.	Verbal Imitation Test
VIII.	Sign Imitation Test

The communication interviews are designed for use with parents, teachers, nurses, care-givers or anyone else who knows the child well. They should be used as a basis for collecting information and examples rather than as a strict checklist. The assessment of Development of Sounds and Imitation is separated from Receptive and Expressive Abilities since it seems reasonable to view sound production and imitative skills as related to the development of communication skills but not necessarily being used in communication. The interviews have a broad-range coverage which concentrates on the less able child.

Expressive and Receptive Vocabulary Tests and the Motor and Verbal Imitation Tests were designed for use with the difficult-to-test child who nonetheless has some abilities. Each section therefore comprises a Pre-Training phase and a Test phase. The argument underlying the use of both procedures is that the child may not be able to demonstrate his abilities because he is not familiar with formal test settings. The first phase in the procedure, the pre-training phase, is designed to teach the child to 'play the game', to attend, and not be disruptive. In this phase the child is first tested over eight trials on an easy problem to see if he plays the game spontaneously. If he does, pre-training is terminated and the test phase follows. If he does not perform adequately on five out of the first eight tasks he is prompted and reinforced for a further block of trials until he has shown correct behaviour on five consecutive trials, or until he completes 32 trials. Trials 33 to 40 are again unprompted and represent the final test trials. Evidence of improvement during the pre-training phase may be taken as some indication of educability in this area.

If the child performs adequately in pre-training he moves on to the test phase. Here again correct responding is rewarded. In each of the components a range of responses is tested on up to three occasions. Specific criteria vary from test to test but in all cases two lists are provided. The second list represents more difficult items than the first. In addition the Expressive and Receptive Vocabulary procedures may be tailored to the individual tested in order to cover material which may have been included in a particular training programme. Procedures for isolating the particular components of a complex stimulus being responded to by the child are outlined. Each of the lists should take approximately 20 minutes to administer. If the session seems to be running much over time it should be terminated and the child given a second test session.

I. Communication Interview — Receptive Abilities

Each of the stems of the lattice relates to a fairly definable activity or skill.

Hears and Listens

C1   Does he respond to any sound?
         Probe: What sounds?

C2   Does he respond to sound within the volume of normal speech? By turning, smiling, startling etc.?
         Probe: What sounds? What does he do?

C3   Does he hit or bang things when he is playing?
         Probe: What does he do?

C4   Does he respond consistently to any sound?
         Probes: Like nursery rhymes . . . Goes to the door on hearing a knock . . . laughs at particular sounds . . . claps to tunes or music. Please state your example.

Understands Need-Related Gestures

C5   Will follow a simple request or command if you take him to the object and prompt him to carry out the response, e.g. take him to a chair and sit him down.

C6   Will respond to smiles or frowns appropriately, i.e. by persisting or stopping.

C7   Will follow request or command if you use gesture, e.g. will come if you hold out your arms and motion him to come to you.

C8   Will follow request or command if you point to the object to be acted on, e.g. pointing to a chair for him to sit down on it.

C9   Will follow gestures *which relates to his needs,* e.g. will show understanding of a mime of drinking from a cup.

Understands Need-Related Words

C10   Understands by intonation the meaning of single words or pairs of words *without* gestures, e.g. 'no' through the sharp intonation, 'yes' through encouraging tone.

C11   Can he respond appropriately to his name?

C12   Understands single words or pair of words *without* gestures and independent of intonation, e.g. 'no', 'stop', 'come here', 'sit down', 'stand up'.

C13   Understands single words, which relate to his needs, e.g. 'drink?', as question from adult to child to see if he wants a drink.

Understands Need Related Non-Fade Symbols

C14   Can play simple matching games using visual cues, e.g. is successful in *visually* directed form board or posting box performance.

C15   Will play with objects and show some spontaneous matching of objects in terms of their surface characteristics, e.g. matches blocks of same size and colour.

C16   Will respond appropriately when asked questions relating to his needs when objects are used, e.g. holding up a cup to ask if he wants a drink or a frying pan for food.

C17   Will respond appropriately when asked need-related questions through pictures or objects, e.g. selection of a specific item from a menu which pictures several alternatives.

C18   Understands when asked need-related questions through the use of line drawings or pictographic symbols.

Understands the Idea of Naming

N.B. All of the following items relate to spoken word, sign and symbol use.

C19   Can he identify common objects which you ask him to get or point to when you name them using *either* signs, symbols or spoken words? For example, shoe, spoon, pencil. The objects should be familiar but not need-related.

C20   Can he identify people he knows well by name? For example, 'where's mummy?'.

C21   Can he point to various parts of his body when they are named by spoken words, signs or symbols? For example, 'show me your nose, mouth, eyes, hair, ear, hand, foot'.

C22   Will show you or go to rooms or parts of the house or school when asked to go through spoken words, signs or symbols.

Understands Descriptive Words

N.B. All of the following items related to spoken word, sign or symbol use.

C23   Does he understand the names of colours? For example, can he show you a red book?

C24   Does he show use of colour in his play? For example, does he sort things into different colours or prefer things of one colour?

C25   Does he understand words concerning size, e.g. big, small, etc?

C26   Does he show use of size in play? For example, does he sort things into different sizes or use inset puzzles or posting boxes which show he knows about size?

C27   Does he understand words which concern shape? For example, can he show you the round or square beads when you ask him?

C28   Does he show use of shape in his play? For example, can he do puzzles or use posting boxes which need him to know about shapes?

C29   Does he understand words about number, one, two, some, all, a lot, etc?

C30   Does he show in his play or other situations that he understands something about number? Can he match pictures with the same number of things on them?

Understands Simple Phrases

N.B. All of the following items relate to spoken word, sign or symbol use.

C31   Can he understand action words when they are applied to himself (spoken words, signs or symbols)? For example does he understand run, walk, lie down, sit up, stand up, look, look up, etc?

C32   Can he understand action words when they are applied to other people?

C33   Can he understand phrases like, 'man sit', 'boy fall', 'Peter hit', etc., where a person or animal and an action are put together?

C34   Can he understand phrases concerning location, e.g. 'cup table', meaning, the cup is on the table, or 'mummy kitchen', 'Mummy is in the kitchen'?

C35   Understands possessives, e.g. 'Teacher's book', 'daddy's hammer', 'Larry's shoe'.

C36   Can he show that he understands prepositions like 'on', 'in', 'under', when these are combined with known words, e.g. 'on table', 'under bed'?

II. Communication Interview — Development of Sounds and Imitation

CS1   Does he ever make coughing, gagging, laughing or crying sounds?

CS2   Does he eat normally, i.e. with adequate control of lips, jaw, tongue and swallowing and at a normal rate?

CS3   Does he produce a variety of different sounds, other than laughing and crying? Detail in terms of vowels and consonants.

CS4   Does he sing when on his own?

CS5   Does he babble, that is, produce 'chains' of sound repetitively, did-did-did, nan-nan, etc., that do not sound like speech but contain the same sound repeated again and again?

CS6   Does he produce varied babbling, i.e. speech sounds which are linked together rather than being repetitive? These may or may not be communicative.

CI1   Can imitate simple motor responses like stirring a spoon round a cup when the response imitated is appropriate to the situation, i.e. stirring liquid in a cup is one thing you do with a spoon.

CI2   Can imitate motor responses like clapping his hands or putting them on his head when the responses are arbitrary.

CI3   Can imitate arbitrary motor responses like turning a cup upside down on top of a box.

CI4   Can imitate his own speech sounds when you repeat them back to him when he is producing sounds.

CI5   Can imitate any single speech sound within his repertoire on request.

CI6   Can imitate pairs of speech sounds, e.g. 'ga', 'bu' which are in his repertoire of combinations.

CI7   Can imitate novel pairs of speech sounds, i.e. ones which he does not habitually combine.

CI88 Can imitate consonant-vowel-consonant sounds.

III. Communication Interview — Expressive Abilities

Basic Needs and Expression

CE1   Does he have clear needs and preferences?

CE2   Does he have a change of facial expression such as smiling, frowning, crying, 'looking angry', etc?

CE3   Does he make eye contact? In other words will he look directly into another person's eyes and show that he is aware of the eye contact.

CE4   When he is happy (that is not crying, busy at play, etc . . .) does he smile in response to a smile directed at him?

CE5   Does he smile in response to any personal approach? For example: will he smile when spoken to and smiled at, when stroked, picked up, rocked, etc.

Asking through Manipulation

CE6   Does he ever reach up to an adult to be lifted?

CE7   Does he guide other people physically so that they do what he wants? For example: places an adult's hand on the door when he wants to go out.

CE8   Does he lead or push a person to something he wants? For example: Pushes adult to where the sweet tin is.

CE9   Does he bring objects to adults and ask to be helped with them?

For example: Places adult's fingers about a container which he wants opened.

CE10   Does he show a near object that he wants by touching? Is this accompanied by demanding noises or a clear request, plus questioning expression, etc.?

CE11   Can signify 'no' by pushing the adult's hand away or pulling the adult away, with or without accompanying noise.

CE12   Can he show you what he wants by pointing to the object when the object is visible?

Asking through Pointing

CE13   Can show you what he wants by touching a related object, either a three-dimensional representation or a picture, when the object which the child wants is visible to him.

CE14   Can show you what he wants by pointing to the location of the object when it is not visible.

CE15   Can show you what he wants by pointing to a representation when he cannot see the object.

Asking through Gestures

CE16   Can use learned signs to indicate that he wants something when it is offered to him.

CE17   Can use learned signs 'spontaneously', i.e. to indicate that he wants something which is not present.

CE18   Demonstrates what he wants by mimes which he has devised either within, or independent of, a sign teaching programme.

CE19   Can he nod to indicate 'yes'?

CE20   Can he shake his head to say 'no'?

Asking through Sounds

CE21   Does he make sounds which indicate that he is happy, sad, etc.?

CE22   Does he make sounds which draw your attention to his needs? For example: being hurt, wanting to go out, etc.?

Descriptive Use of Single Words

CE23   Can use single spoken words, signs or symbols when asked to name objects or people.

CE24   Can use single spoken words, signs or symbols 'spontaneously' to draw attention to them, the equivalent of 'look, there is a bus'.

CE25   Can use a spoken word, sign or symbol to ask for recurrence, e.g. 'more', 'again'.

CE26   Can use a spoken word, sign or symbol to indicate 'no'.

CE27   Can use single spoken words, signs or symbols to name pictures.

CE28   Can use action words either in speech, sign or symbols to describe his own actions, e.g. 'draw', when drawing.

CE29   Can use action words either spoken, signed or through symbols to describe the actions of adults or other children, e.g. 'run' when sees another child running.

Use of Phrases (spoken words, signs or symbols)

CE30   Can ask for more or again using a two-word phrase, e.g. 'more drink', 'swing again'.

CE31   Can indicate 'no' with a two-word phrase, e.g. 'no bed', 'no bath'.

CE32   Can use two-word phrases to describe the actions of others which he sees either directly or in pictures.

CE33   Can use words appropriately as adjectives, e.g. 'red book', 'big man'.

IV. Expressive Vocabulary Test

N.B. Since certain objects are common to the Expressive and Receptive Vocabulary the Expressive Vocabulary assessment should always be given first.

The basic test procedure suggested here involves the child in labelling 15 objects. The procedure includes two phases. The first is a pre-training phase which ensures that the child is familiar with the method of presentation and demands of the situation or, for children who are not used to such tasks, teaches the child how to 'play the game'. The Test Phase tests the child's ability to label.

The procedure can be used to check initial knowledge of words, signs, or symbols to be taught in a teaching programme, to assess progress in such programmes, or to identify the aspect of a complex stimulus to which the child may be responding. The basic Pre-Training and Test procedures will be outlined initially. Modifications of the procedure will then be outlined.

PRE-TRAINING PHASE

Two pre-training objects are selected. In the standard spoken word procedure these are a milk bottle (bottle) and a realistic plastic flower (flower). The examiner says '. . . look', simultaneously placing either the bottle or the flower on the table. When the child looks, the examiner says 'What is this?' In order to succeed at the pre-training phase the child must:

(a) look at the stimulus object;
(b) name correctly on five consecutive trials.

PRE-TRAINING SCORE SHEET

Correct orientation to the object and responding verbally should be rewarded. It may be necessary to prompt responses initially in the pre-training phase. As soon as the child produces five consecutive responses within forty pre-training trials the pre-training phase should be terminated and the test phase not attempted. Trials 1-8 are unprompted, 9-32 prompted shaping trials, 33-40 unprompted assessment trials.

TEST PHASE

During the test phase only correct identification of the object should be rewarded.

Procedure

The steps in the procedure are as follows:

1. Object held in front of the child.
2. Say ' . . .look' indicating the object.
3. As soon as the child looks at the object say 'what is the name of this?' whilst pointing to the object.
4. Repeat steps 2 and 3 once more after 10 seconds if no attention or response.
5. If the child responds correctly, reward immediately. If inappropriately remove the object without comment.
6. If the child does not respond during ten seconds after the second request remove the object and record no response.
7. Correct responses are recorded C; no response is recorded N; incorrect responses are scored I; disruptive responses are scored D; approximations to the correct word should be coded A and the form noted.
8. If prompts are given during the pre-training phase these should be recorded and coded P.

TEST SCORE SHEET
Use with Spoken Words

The procedures may be used in order to assess the child's speech in several ways. Standard pre-training procedures and the standard list of 15 objects may be used in conjunction with the record form. The record form contains two lists (1 and 2). List 2 words are, overall, more difficult than List 1. Within each list there are three repeats of the same 15 items in different orders. Users may wish to set their own criteria but if the child is successful completely with any column of a list all objects will have been correctly named. This listing presentation condition can be varied in three ways:

(a)   Presentation of the objects themselves including miniatures of the larger objects. This will assess the child's responsiveness to three-dimensional objects. Eight of the objects can be presented in full size versions, block, ball, hammer, cup, hat, watch, clock and apple, the others in model form. This may give interesting information in itself when responses to full size objects are compared to those of models.

(b)   Presentation of colour photographs of the objects to assess the child's responsiveness to two-dimensional representations with colour cues.

(c)   Presentation of line drawings of the objects. It is possible that some children will perform at a higher level with line drawings than colour photographs since distracting cues are likely to be eliminated in line drawings.

Individualized Use.

Instead of using the standard list users may wish to develop their own lists for Pre-training and Test Phases. The procedures can then be used to check progress within teaching programmes. For this purpose blank record sheets are available (pages 178 to 179). Users may wish to follow the randomization indicated on the standard Pre-training and Test protocols.

When individualized lists are used it is clearly possible to assess using any of the three levels of representation outlined above.

Use with Manual Signs

The procedures may be readily adapted for use with children who have learned manual signing. Minor adaptations may be made to the procedure for administering the tests by inclusion of signed instructions in steps 2 and 3 and signed reward in step 5.

The child's responses may be either in sign or, for some children, speech or speech approximation may be added in. Note may be taken if and when this occurs.

Assessment of Responsiveness to Aspects of the Stimulus
Complex Used in Teaching

As we noted in our chapter on use and interpretation, procedures are required which can assess the child's responsiveness to speech or speech related phenomena, and to presentation of an object for children who have been taught by a Total Communication method. Total Communication teaching usually involves teaching the child to use a sign in a situation in which the object is shown *and* the spoken name of the object is given with prompting (if necessary) of the appropriate sign. This procedure leads to a situation in which the child may be responding to either the spoken word *or* the movement of the teacher's lips as the word is spoken *or* the appearance of the object if a simple procedure is used.

The modifications to the standard procedure which allow us to assess these effects are easy to devise. Four methods can be used:

(a) *Sound only.* The word is spoken whilst the examiner covers his or her mouth so that the child cannot see the lips move. The object is *not* presented. This assesses response to the *sound* of the spoken word. The occurrence of a sign and its correctness is recorded.

(b) *Lip Movements only.* The word is mouthed silently, the object is *not* presented. This assesses responsiveness to lip movements. Again the sign mode, if any, is recorded.

(c) *Object only.* The object is held up without the examiner saying anything. This procedure evaluates the effect of the object in eliciting signs. Signs, if any, are recorded.

(d) *Sounds plus Lip Movements plus Object.* It is possible that the child is responding to different aspects of the stimulus complex for different signs. Consequently it is sensible to evaluate responsiveness to the whole complex, holding up the object and speaking its name in such a way that the child can see the examiner's mouth. Comparison of performance under this condition with previous conditions will allow an evaluation of the relative contribution of the elements.

For all conditions the instruction at step 3 of the standard procedure may need to be modified to what sign for ... followed by either the word, silent word or pointing to or holding up the object.

Clearly other variants of the procedure may be used as with responsiveness to words. Objects may be represented three-dimensionally or two-dimensionally and standard or individualized lists may be used.

The standard procedures should be followed as far as repetitions of the request, reward and non-reward, termination of trials and recording of responses.

Use with Symbols

Adaptations of the procedures for use with visual symbols require one or two additional adaptations. The main difference between expressive vocabulary assessment with spoken words or signs and with symbols is that spoken words and signs have to be recalled from memory whereas symbols have only to be selected, recognized, from a set which the child normally has in front of him or at least readily accessible. This means that we have to decide how many symbols the child is to have access to when he or she is tested.

The decision on number of symbols will depend very much on the child's level of knowledge. If the equivalent of the standard procedure is being used we would suggest that the child is given the 15 appropriate symbols plus up to five 'distractors', symbols for which objects will not be presented. This will act as a control by cutting down the influence of guessing. Similar procedures can be used if the child has an individualized list. Clearly, for some children, individualized lists will be shorter than 15 items.

Assessment of Response to Aspects of the Stimulus Complex used in Teaching

As with sign teaching symbols are often taught through use of a Total Communication method. We can assess the degree to which the spoken word, lip-movements and object presentation are influential by procedures paralleling those described for sign. Again four methods can be used:

(a) *Sound only*. The word is spoken, following the request 'Show me symbol for . . . ' or 'what symbol for . . . ', whilst the examiner covers his or her mouth to prevent lip-reading. The object is *not* shown. The symbols indicated, if any, are recorded.

(b) *Lip Movements only*. The word is mouthed silently following the request. The object is *not* presented. Symbol choice is recorded if it occurs.

(c) *Object only*. The object is held up following the request 'show me the symbol for . . . ' or 'what symbol for . . . ' The word is *not* spoken. Symbol choice is recorded, if it occurs.

(d) *Sound plus Lip Movement plus Object.* The object is held up following the request, 'show me the symbol for . . .' with the word spoken in such a way that the child can see the examiner's lip movements. Symbol choice is recorded if it occurs.

The standard procedure is followed as far as repetitions of the request, reward and non-reward, termination of trials and recording of responses.

V. Receptive Vocabulary Test

The basic procedures for assessment of receptive vocabulary parallel those described for expressive vocabulary assessment. Again there is a Pre-training Phase and a Test Phase, the function of the Pre-training phase being to assess the child's ability to understand the game and, in certain cases, to teach him the expected structure of the game.

Ten objects are used in List 1 of the standard form of the procedure. Six of these: ball, cup, car, watch, clock and apple, are also used in the Expressive Vocabulary List 1. Scissors and pencil appear in List 2 of the Expressive Vocabulary. One of the List 2 Receptive Vocabulary words, hat, appears in the Expressive Vocabulary List 1. Eight further words appear in List 2 Expressive Vocabulary: chair, book, telephone, table, box, shoe, glass and sock.

As with the Expressive Vocabulary the procedures can be used to check initial knowledge of words, signs or symbols to be used in teaching programmes, to assess progress in such programmes or to identify the particular component of a stimulus complex which is being attended to by a child. The basic procedures will be outlined initially and modifications will then be described.

PRE-TRAINING PHASE

The child is required to respond appropriately to instructions by selecting one out of two objects given repeated testing. The purpose of this phase is to ensure that the child produces appropriate selection responses by pointing and reaching for or otherwise indicating a choice. Appropriate selection responses should be encouraged by placing the items apart so that they can not be picked up simultaneously by one hand. If the child has a tendency to reach for both objects, one with each hand, the non-preferred hand should be gently restrained. Responses may be prompted in order to initiate them. Criterion behaviour in the pre-training phase is correct choice on five consecutive trials. All correct choices should be rewarded. If the child does not reach the criterion within 40 trials, the session is terminated and the test phase is not attempted. Trials 1-8 are unprompted trials, 9-32 prompted shaping trials, 33-40 unprompted trials.

TEST PHASE

There are several variants of the test phase procedures. These will be described after the basic procedure has been detailed.

Basic Procedure

The child is seated either beside the examiner or opposite him in such a position that pairs of objects or pictures can be presented simultaneously. If material reward is to be used it may be valuable to arrange the setting in such a way that objects or cards cover 'wells' in which incentives can be concealed out of sight of the child before each trial. The steps on each trial are as follows:

1. Objects placed in boxes on either side of the child out of his reach but in full sight.
2. Examiner says or signs 'Look . . . give me the . . .'
3. Examiner pushes boxes toward child repeating, 'give me the . . . ' Boxes are put in a position where the child cannot reach both simultaneously with one hand. Make sure not to cue the child on the correct response by looking at the named object. Either look directly at the child's eyes or at a fixed point on the table.
4. The boxes are left for 10 seconds. If the child has not responded within this time record no response. (NR).
5. If the child responds appropriately reinforce immediately. Incorrect responses are ignored. Both objects are withdrawn as soon as possible after recording has occurred. Form of response is recorded as correct —C, No response — NR or Incorrect — I.

Use with Spoken Words

The procedures can be used in the standard way using spoken words without signs or gestures. If this is done there are several variants which may throw particular light on the child's abilities. These procedures parallel those for the Expressive Vocabulary assessment.
(a)   Presentation of *actual objects* or miniatures of objects. This variant assesses the child's ability to identify three dimensional objects.
(b)   *Coloured photographs* or pictures of relevant objects may be used.
(c)   *Line drawings* of relevant objects will allow assessment of

responsiveness when colour cues, which may be distracting, have been eliminated.

Individualized Use

The two lists provided may not be appropriate for use with children in programmes where there is a need to assess vocabulary. In order to allow for users who wish to develop their own lists blank Pre-Training and Test protocols are included. Users may wish to follow the randomization used in the original lists. As with the standard lists children being assessed on the individualized lists can be tested with objects, colour pictures, and line drawings.

Use with Manual Signs

Children in sign programmes are normally taught through Total Communication methods in which teachers speak and sign the names of objects. This may mean that the child will learn to respond to speech or some speech related phenomenon, signs or both. The particular aspect of the stimulus complex which the child is responding to can be assessed through minor amendments to the basic Receptive Vocabulary assessment procedure. Four methods can be used

(a) *Sound only.* In order to assess if the child is responding to the sound of a word the instructions in steps 2 and 3 of the procedures could be spoken and, if required, simultaneously signed with the mouth covered when the name of the object is spoken.

(b) *Lip Movements only.* The steps 2 and 3 instructions are spoken and, if required, simultaneously signed with the test word mouthed but not signed. Ensure that the child is looking at you when you mouth the word.

(c) *Sign only.* The instructions in step 2 and 3 are spoken and possibly signed with the test word signed without the spoken word.

(d) *Speech plus Lip Movements plus Sign.* In this condition the step 2 and 3 procedures are spoken and, if necessary, signed, with the object name being spoken in full view of the child and signed at the same time.

Clearly, responsiveness to sign and other variants can be assessed with objects, colour pictures or line drawings. Procedures for assessing non-responding and reward are followed as in the standard procedure.

Use with Symbols

Adaptation for use with symbols requires little change from the procedures for signing. Steps 2 and 3 adapted to include symbols for objects, and possibly instructions, rather than signs. Since most symbol teaching involves a variant of Total Communication, speech is presumed to be used in the instructions. Again four variants of the basic procedure can be used to assess how the child is responding to the stimulus complex of symbol plus speech.

(a) *Sound only.* Instructions in Steps 2 and 3 are spoken, and, if appropriate, expressed in symbols, with the name of the object being spoken by the examiner with his or her mouth covered.

(b) *Lip Movements only.* Step 2 and 3 instructions are spoken and, if appropriate, expressed in symbols. The name of the object is mouthed silently by the examiner.

(c) *Symbol only.* Instructions are given in speech and symbol if appropriate. The name of the object is expressed through a symbol without the spoken name being given.

(d) *Speech plus Lip Movement plus Sign.* The instructions and name of the object are spoken and expressed in symbols.

Standard procedures should be followed for other steps in the administration of the Receptive Vocabulary test.

VI. Motor Imitation Test
PRE-TRAINING PHASE
Two simple responses are taught to the child. These are to squeak a toy and to drop a bead into a cup. The objectives of the pre-training phase are to:

(1) Get the child to attend to the model.
(2) Get the child to imitate the responses appropriately.
(3) To eliminate other responses to the setting.

The pre-training phase is terminated when the child has imitated successfully on five consecutive trials without prompts. The first eight trials are assessment trials. If imitation is not shown the responses are shaped until trial 32, trials 33–40 are then unprompted assessments.

All correct responses and approximate responses during the earlier stage of response shaping are rewarded.

If the child does not reach criterion within 40 trials the test phase is omitted.

TEST PHASE
The test phase consists of two levels. Level 1 responses are all high

probability responses given the stimulus objects. All are object-oriented fine motor responses. Level 2 responses are either object- or body-oriented responses. In each category there are fine and gross responses.

All correct responses are rewarded.

Procedure

The child and tester are seated side by side at a table.

1. If objects are used, examiner puts the relevant object on the table in front of the subject and, if specified, a second object in front of himself. Pre-responding is prevented and the model is not presented until the child has not pre-responded for five seconds.

2. E says 'Look . . . ' (child's name) and points to either himself or the relevant object.

3. As soon as the child looks in the correct direction E says 'Do this' and then models the response.

4. Ten seconds are allowed to elapse for the child to respond. If he does not respond steps 2 and 3 are repeated once. Inappropriate responses e.g. throwing, terminate the trial, again steps 2 and 3 should be repeated once.

5. If the child does not respond during the second ten second period the trial is terminated and the objects withdrawn.

6. Responses are recorded as correct if criterion is reached and coded +. No response is recorded N, approximate responses should be briefly described and coded A. Inappropraite responses are scored I. If child makes one or more responses within a trial before the correct one note form of these responses as fully as possible.

During the pre-training phase responses may be prompted or physically guided. Criterion responses in the pre-training phase and in the test phase should be rewarded. Other responses are ignored.

If the child gets nine out of ten trials on Level 1 correct go on to Level 2 immediately. If the child gets nine out of ten trials of Level 2 correct, terminate the trial.

Motor Imitation
PRE-TRAINING
Definitions

1. *Squeaky toy:* Examiner applies pressure to toy with hand producing squeaking noise.
Equipment: Two squeaky toys.

2. *Drop bead in cup:* The examiner picks up bead and releases it into

cup from a height of 5 cms or more above top of cup.
Equipment: Two cups — two wooden beads.

LEVEL 1
Definitions
1. *Ring bells:* The examiner picks up bell and shakes it so that sound is produced. One bell used by examiner, one by child. The examiner demonstrates the correct response for 10 seconds. The child must pick up the bell and ring it to score.

2. *Stack blocks:* Examiner picks up one block and places it on top of another. Examiner models with his own blocks and leaves model. The child must reproduce the model to score.

3. *Roll ball:* Examiner rolls ball at least 30 cms in such a way that it maintains contact with surface of table. The child is given another ball and must roll it to score.

4.*Cup in cup:* The examiner picks up smaller of two graduated cups and inserts it, right side up, into larger cup. The child has two other cups.

5. *Put on hat:* The examiner picks up hat and places it on top of his head. Examiner models with one hat leaving the hat on after modelling for duration of item.

6. *Stir with spoon:* The examiner picks up spoon by handle and moves it round inside cup. Two spoons, two cups. Stir for 10 seconds.Definite circular stirring for two seconds required for correct response to be scored.

7. *Push car:* The examiner pushes car and releases it in such a way as to make it travel at least 30 cms on the table surface. Different cars used by examiner and child. The child must produce 30 cms of travel also.

8. *Beat tambourine:* The examiner holds drumstick in his hand and strikes the upper surface of the tambourine producing a sound. Examiner and child use different tambourines and drumsticks. The examiner demonstrates the response for 10 seconds.

9. *Pull truck:*The examiner grasps the string and pulls the toy across a surface for a distance of at least 30 cms. Examiner and child use different toys. The child must pull for 30 cms to score.

10. *Put on bracelet:* The examiner puts bracelet on either arm at least to the wrist. Examiner and child use different bracelets. The child's bracelet must go to the wrist to score.

LEVEL 2
Definitions

1. *Pull comb through hair:* Examiner places comb on table, one in front of the child and one in front of himself. He says '(Timmy) look — do this' and proceeds to draw his comb through his hair, either from back to front of head or vice versa. This modelling should last 15 seconds. Any pre-response on the part of the child should be terminated. Examiner looks at child during model. To score the child should pick up the comb and move it across hair.

2. *Hands on top of head:* Examiner says '(Timmy) look — do this'. When child attends, the examiner puts his hands on top of his head, palms down and elbows parallel to shoulders. The model should be maintained for ten seconds. Examiner looks at the child whilst modelling. To score, the child's hand should touch the top of his head.

3. *Rubs hands together:* Examiner should give the command '(Timmy) look — do this'. The model's hand should be held in a praying position and should be rubbed up and down with a well-defined action. The model should continue for 10 seconds. Any form of hand-rubbing response is acceptable. Examiner looks at child during model.

4. *Draw a line:* Examiner should place a large sheet of white paper on the table in front of the child. He should give the command '(Timmy) look —do this', and draw a heavy pencil, crayon or felt-pen line about 10 cms long from side to side across the paper. The pen should then be put at the right side of the paper. Any mark on the paper scores. Time limit 15 seconds.

5. *Put block in box:* Examiner says '(Timmy) look — do this'. When child attends he picks up a block and places it in the box. Child has his own block and box. Allow the child ten seconds to respond. The child must put the block in his box or in the examiner's.

6. *Slap thighs:* Examiner says '(Timmy) look — do this'. Whilst seated examiner raises his hands about 30 cms above thighs and slaps them with both hands together repeatedly about once per second for ten seconds. At least three thigh slaps with one or both hands are needed to score. The child's manner of imitating the movement should be noted, with one hand or two, and if one, which hand.

7. *Raise one arm:* Examiner says '(Timmy) look — do this'. Whilst seated examiner raises his right arm above his head and holds it there for ten seconds. Raising either arm above the shoulder for three seconds is an acceptable level to score.

8. *Blow whistle:* Examiner says '(Timmy) look — do this'. Examiner

then picks up whistle and blows it once every three seconds for ten seconds. The child has his own whistle and must blow at least once to score.

9. *Finger on nose:* Examiner says '(Timmy) look — do this.' Examiner then places his right index finger on the tip of his nose. Position held for ten seconds. The child must place any finger on his nose or his face round his nose to score.

10. *Pick up block:* Two blocks are placed on the floor between examiner and child. Examiner says '(Timmy) look — do this'. Examiner then picks up one block and puts it in front of him on the table. Child given ten seconds to respond. The child must pick up one block and put it on the table.

VII. Verbal Imitation Test

PRE-TRAINING
All responses should be tape recorded.
   The obejctives of the pre-training phase are to:
   (1) Get the child to attend to the sound to be imitated.
   (2) Get the child to produce the correct response.
   (3) Get the response to an audible level.

The examiner should get the child's attention, look directly at him and then say 'Say a' or 'Say mmm'. Repeat after ten seconds if the child does not respond. If the child does not respond after a second ten second period, mark the trial as N (no response); if the response is incorrect but intelligible, record the response; if the child's reponse is unintelligible, record it as UT. If the child was attending by looking at the tester but does not respond record + in the Attention column. Reward the child for correct responses or approximations of correct responses on pre-criterion trials. The pre-training phase is terminated when the child correctly imitates on five successive trials. The first eight trials are unprompted assessment trials. If the child does not reach criterion within these trials, his behaviour is shaped to trial 32. Trials 33–40 are again unprompted trials.
   If the criterion is not reached in 40 trials the test phase may be omitted.

TEST PHASE
All responses should be tape recorded.
   The basic procedure is the same as in the pre-training phase.

Examiner calls the child's attention and then says 'Say . . . ' (the appropriate sound). If there is no response within ten seconds repeat and give a further ten second period.

Correct responses are rewarded and coded +, incorrect are ignored and coded —. No response coded N, incorrect but intelligible responses are recorded, unintelligible responses recorded UT.

If the child scores nine out of ten responses correct on the first column of Level 1 go on directly to Level 2. If the child scores nine out of ten in the first column of Level 2 terminate.

VIII. Sign Imitation Test (SIT)

The test is designed for use with children who are either in sign language programmes or who are being considered for placement in such programmes. The child would sensibly be assessed on the Motor Imitation Test before assessment with the current procedure.

The procedure comprises five components. These may be administered in order within a single session or in separate sessions. Once Hand Preference has been established (Section 1) the order of administration of subsequent sections is not critical although it would seem sensible to administer the Hand Postures component before the Combinations section. The order in which the sections are presented was used in test standardization and analysis.

SECTION 1: HAND PREFERENCE

The section involves three activites, picking up a small reward, reaching out to hold the examiner's hand and imitating a pencil drawing. The first two activities are repeated twice.

The purpose of the procedure is to identify which hand should be used to model responses in Sections 2, 4 and 5 of the SIT.

Equipment

Two small rewards/incentives known to be liked by the subject, e.g. two small sweets, or one incentive e.g. a favourite toy car, which can be presented twice. A pencil, felt or nylon-tipped pen and piece of A4 paper.

Procedure

The subject and examiner are seated opposite one another at a table approximately 1 metre wide. The subject's mid-line is noted.

1. The subject's attention is called 'look . . .' with the incentive being held up in the examiner's right hand. The incentive is then placed on the table at the subject's mid-line and 30 cms in front of him.

Record which hand is used to take the incentive.

2. The examiner calls the subject, 'Look . . . ' if he or she is not looking at the examiner. The examiner then holds out his right hand to the subject's mid-line, 30 cms in front of the subject whilst saying 'Give me your hand'. The hand which the child uses or uses first is noted.

3. The examiner puts a piece of paper on the table 30 cms in front of the subject and at the mid-line. The examiner calls the subject's attention 'Look . . . ' and then draws a pencil line down the paper beginning at the subject's edge of the paper. The pencil is then put on the line at right angles to the line at the examiners end of the line. The subject is told 'You draw'. The hand used to pick up the pencil or pen is noted. Note also if the subject changes hands.

4. As 2 but examiner offers his *left* hand.

5. As 1 but the incentive is put down by the examiner with his or her *left* hand.

The purpose of the test is to determine which hand the subject prefers. As a consequence the 'majority' hand is taken. Hand preference may be unstable from day-to-day so it may be necessary to re-determine preference if there is a time-lapse between sections.

If the RIGHT HAND is preferred the EXAMINER SITS ON THE SUBJECT'S LEFT and models postures with his RIGHT HAND just to the left of the subjects's mid-line in Sections 2, 4 and 5.

If the LEFT HAND is preferred the EXAMINER SITS ON THE SUBJECT'S RIGHT and models postures with the LEFT HAND just to the right of the subject's mid-line in Sections 2, 4 and 5.

SECTION 2: HAND POSTURES (See also pp. 143-6)

In this section the 12 hand postures are modelled for the subject to imitate. The 12 postures and acceptable and unacceptable alternatives are illustrated in Figure 1 in their order of presentation. The critical features of the hand postures used in this section and in the combinations sections are as follows:

1. *Flat hand (Fh)* (American Sign Language, ASL, B): The fingers should be together, straight from the hand. Curvature of fingers between fingers and palm should not exceed 20°. Separation of fingers to the position where 4f and 1f are parallel represents the maximum acceptable separation. Thumb position is not critical but it should be held close to the first finger.

2. *Scoop Hand (Sch)* (ASL, B, fingers curved): The fingers must be

together. Maximum acceptable curvature is to the point where nails are parallel to palm (cf. small C Hand). The thumb should be close to the first finger.

3. *Compressed Hand (Coh)* (ASL, Flat O): The tips of the fingers and thumb should meet; *N.B.* the instructions illustrate *unacceptable* alternatives only.

4. *Index Hand (Ih)* (ASL, G): The critical feature is the extension of the straight 1f from the curved 2f, 3f, 4f. The thumb should be at approximately 30° from the first finger.

5. *First and Second Finger Hand (1, 2fh)* (ASL,H): The defining feature is the extension of straight, parallel 1f and 2f from the curved 3f and 4f. Thumb position is not critical but should cross the palm.

6. *V Hand (Vh)* (ASL,K): If 1 and 2f are extended straight and separated but must be parallel to back of hand. Thumb position is not critical but should cross the palm.

7. *O Hand (Oh)* (ASL, O): The critical feature is the creation of an O by bringing together the thumb and equally curved fingers.

8. *Closed Fist Hand (CFih)* (ASL,A): Fingers may touch at base of fingers or on palm. Thumb position is not critical but should not be held rigidly at right angles to the hand.

9. *Right Angle Index Hand (RtAIh):* The critical features here are that the 1f is bent at 45° to 90° to the back of the hand with 2f, 3f and 4f curved on hand. Thumb position is not critical but should touch the fingers.

10. *Paget L Hand (PLh)* (ASL,B, fingers straight): The critical feature is that all fingers are held touching at an angle between 45° and 90° to the back of the hand. Thumb position is not critical but should not be held out rigidly at right angles.

11. *Y Hand (Yh)* (ASL,Y): The critical feature is the extension of the thumb and 4f from curved 1,2 and 3f.

2. *Crossed, Second, Third and Fourth Fingerhand (C2, 3, 4fh)* (ASL, S): The critical features are the extension of 2,3 and 4f with 1f curved. Thumb position is not critical but should not be held out rigidly at right angles.

Procedure 1. Examiner says 'Look . . .' at the same time tapping the table to get the subject's attention. The instruction is repeated three times at approximately three second intervals if the subject does not respond. If the subject does not attend after these repetitions a mark is recorded in the 'no attention' column of the score sheet and the next item is tried.

2. If the subject responds the examiner says 'do this' and models the posture. All postures are presented with the palm up and angled slightly toward the mid-line of the examiner's body so that the wrist is not straining. If the subject looks but does not respond with an attempted response within three seconds on item 1, (Flat hand), the examiner says 'Put your hand like this' and physically prompts the correct response. If prompts are used the child is not credited with the response but it is modelled again at the end of the sequence. Following item 1, if the subject does not respond within three seconds the experimenter says 'Put your hand like this', once, maintains the posture for three seconds, relaxes and says 'good' and proceeds to the next item. Under these circumstances the child scores the 'no response' column on the score sheet.

3. Correct responses are recorded as such. Incorrect responses or acceptable alternatives should be coded with the letter or letters corresponding to the posture if it is included on the score sheet. If no suitable match is provided a brief description can be made on the score sheet. All responses are rewarded.

SECTION 3. COMBINATIONS (See also p. 147)

Here the subject is presented with signs involving both hands adopting postures. As with Section 2 the first response is prompted if necessary and, if prompted, is repeated after the final sign is modelled. Procedures for ascertaining attention and non-responding are as for Section 2.

Form of sign and sequence is shown on the score sheet.

SECTION 4. PALM DIRECTIONS

The purpose of this section is to see if the subject can imitate palm directions used in signs. All five items use the Flat hand. The variation in location of the hand in respect of the body is necessary if straining is not to be a problem. The procedure is as follows:

1. With positioning of examiner and subject as before the examiner says 'look . . . do this' and then models the response as before. Procedures for prompting, repetition and decision on non-response are as before.

2. Each response is presented only once, with the exception of the first in the case of prompting. Details of responses are as follows for RIGHT handed presentation:

	Palm facing:	Fingers pointing:	Location
1. Flat Hand	Left	Away from body	Opposite lower right ribs.
2. Flat Hand	Away from body	Up	Opposite right shoulder.
3. Flat Hand	Left	Up	Opposite right shoulder.
4. Flat Hand	Up	Away from body	Opposite lower right ribs.
5. Flat Hand	Down	Away from body	Opposite lower right ribs.

If LEFT handed presentation is being used the palm will face *right* in items 1 and 3.

SECTION 5. MOVEMENT

The procedures for determining non-response and other categories parallel those used previously. As in the previous item the hand is held in the Flat Hand position but the child is not scored as in error if he or she uses a different hand posture. The ten movements are selected as being used in sign languages. They are defined as follows:

1. *Out.* The right hand is placed on the centre of mid-chest. It is then moved directly at right angles to chest to full extent of the arm.

2. *Up.* The right hand is held at rest position on the table at the examiner's mid-line. The hand is then raised above head to full extent of the arm.

3. *Supination — Pronation.* Hand held in front of chest in line with the lower ribs and with the elbow at 90°, palm facing upwards. The hand is then turned over and back twice in about five seconds.

4. *Side to side.* Right hand held in line with right shoulder, at mid-chest level. The hand is then moved to left until the hand is to the left of the chest and then returned to right hand side. Repeat twice with two seconds between responses. Opposite instructions hold for left-handed presentation.

5. *Movement of wrist and fingers.* The right or left hand is held with palm upward and the fingers relaxed. The fingers are 'wriggled' each finger being moved independently back and forward for five seconds.

6. *Down.* The hand is held at rest palm down on the table at the examiner's mid-line. The hand is then raised to mid-chest level, moved down below waist level and returned to the rest position.

7. *Circular movements.* Both hands are held, palms facing, at mid-chest level. The hands are then moved reciprocally with circular movement such that each hand draws a circle at right angles to the body. This is a movement like pedalling a bicycle. The movement is continued for around five seconds.

8. *Movement of wrist.* The hand is held in line with the shoulders, palm facing in, and at mid-chest level. The hand is then flapped at the wrist for five seconds.

9. *In.* The hand is held at the mid-line with the elbow extended. The hand is then brought to the chest so that the hand finally touches the mid-chest.

10. *Movement at elbow.* The arm is held with elbow at right angles to upper arm. The arm is then bent at the elbow so as to bring the hand to the shoulder, and then extended and bent again, twice more.

Sign Imitation Test (SIT)

Summary Score Sheet

Name of subject _____

AGE_____SEX_____DATE OF TEST____

WHERE TESTED _____

SCHOOL ETC _____

HAND PREFERENCE Totals   Left_____Right_____

	Correct	No attn.	No resp.
Section Two Postures			
Section Three combinations L _____ R			
Section Four Direction			
Section Five movements			

Comments:

Section One — Hand Preference

Hand Used by Subject

	Left	Right
1. Incentive		
2. Take hand		
3. Drawing		
4. Take hand		
5. Incentive		

Total   Left   Right

Section Two — Hand Postures

Sign	Correct	No attn.	No resp.	Circle Hand Used in Presentation L R Incorrect Response (Specify)
1 Fh				
2 Sch				
3 Coh				
4 Ih				
5 1,2fh				
6 Vh				
7 Oh				
8 CFih				
9 RtAIh				
10 PLh				
11 Yh				
12 C2,3,4fh				
Totals				

Section Three — Combinations

	Sign L	Sign R	Correct L	Correct R	No attn	No resp.	Incorrect Response
1	Fh	Fh					
2	Fh	CFih					
3	Ih	Ih					
4	Fh	Coh					
5	CFih	CFih					
6	Fh	Ih					
7	PLh	PLh					
8	Ih	Oh					
9	Fh	Vh					
10	Oh	Fh					

Totals   L ____R ____Attn.____Resp. ___

Section Four — Palm Direction

Circle Hand Used
in Presentation
L   R

	Direction			Correct	No attn.	No resp.	Incorrect Response (Specify)
1	Fh	L/R	A	LR			
2	Fh	A	U	Sh			
3	Fh	L/R	U	Sh			
4	Fh	U	A	LR			
5	Fh	D	A	LR			

Totals _____ _____ _____

Section Five — Movements

Circle hand used
in Presentation
L   R

	Movement	Correct	No attn.	No resp.	Incorrect Response (Specify)
1	Out				
2	Up				
3	Sup-pron				
4	Side-side				
5	Wrist-fingers				
6	Down				
7	Circle				
8	Wrist				
9	In				
10	Elbow				
	Totals				

Instructions for Administration of the Sign Imitation Test

(see pp. 135-6 for Section 1, *Hand Preference;* pp. 138-9 for Section 4, *Palm Directions;* pp. 139-40 for Section 5, *Movement.*)

Section Two — Hand Postures
All palm to opposite side and up, fingers away.

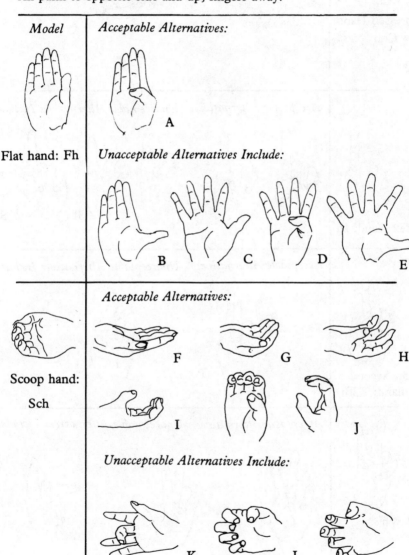

Model	Acceptable Alternatives:
	A
Flat hand: Fh	Unacceptable Alternatives Include:
	B C D E

Acceptable Alternatives:

F   G   H

Scoop hand:

Sch

I   J

Unacceptable Alternatives Include:

K   L

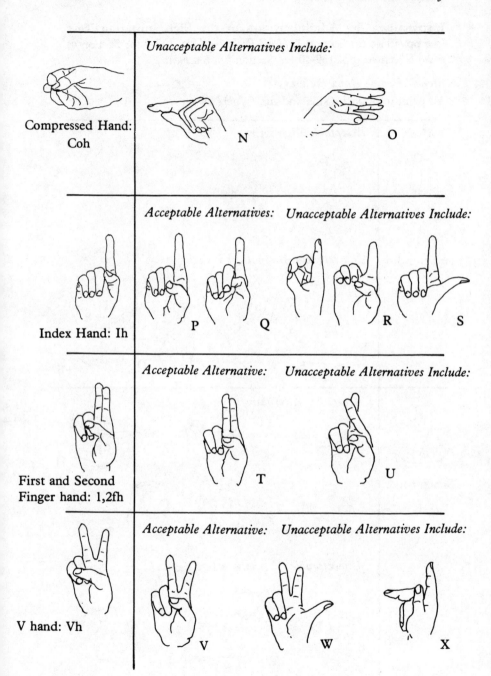

Compressed Hand: Coh

Unacceptable Alternatives Include:

N   O

Index Hand: Ih

Acceptable Alternatives: *Unacceptable Alternatives Include:*

P   Q   R   S

First and Second Finger hand: 1,2fh

Acceptable Alternative: *Unacceptable Alternatives Include:*

T   U

V hand: Vh

Acceptable Alternative: *Unacceptable Alternatives Include:*

V   W   X

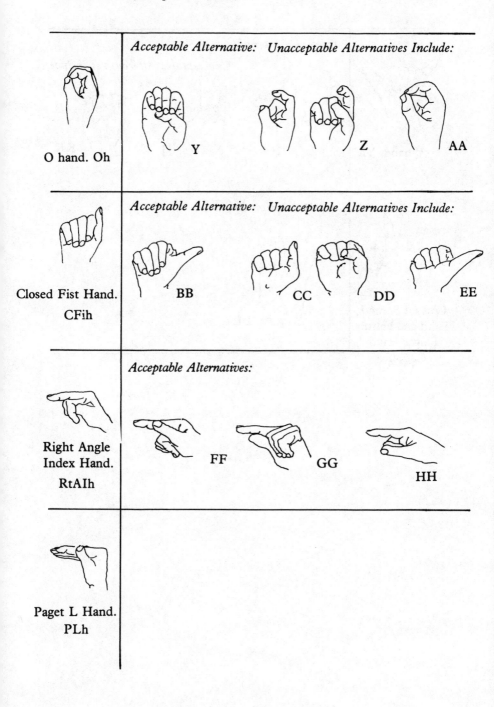

	Acceptable Alternative:	Unacceptable Alternatives Include:
O hand. Oh	Y	Z AA
Closed Fist Hand. CFih	BB	CC DD EE
Right Angle Index Hand. RtAIh	Acceptable Alternatives: FF GG HH	
Paget L Hand. PLh		

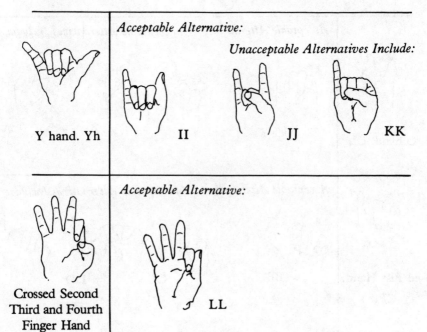

Y hand. Yh

Acceptable Alternative:

Unacceptable Alternatives Include:

II   JJ   KK

Crossed Second
Third and Fourth
Finger Hand
(C2,3,4fh)

Acceptable Alternative:

LL

Section Two — Combinations

All located at lower ribs

Left	Right

Fh   *Fh*

Both palms up and to opposite side, fingers away, hands touch at inner edge of palm.

Fh   *CFih*

Left hand palm up and right, fingers away and right; Right hand palm up, fingers away and left. *Back* of right hand on palm of left.

Ih   *Ih*

Palms up, fingers away, hands touch at inner edges of palms.

Fh   *Coh*

Left hand, palm up fingers away and right; right hand, palm down and toward, fingers away and left. Fingers of right hand on centre of left palm.

CFih   *CFih*

Palms up, fingers away, touching at inner edges of palms.

Fh   *Ih*

Left hand, palm up, fingers away and right; right hand, palm down, fingers away and left. First finger of right hand on centre of left palm.

PLh   *PLh*

Both hands palms to opposite sides, fingers away. Hands touch at tips of 2f and 3f.

Ih   *Oh*

Left hand palm up, fingers away and to right; right hand palm left, fingers away; Back of 1f of left hand on O of right hand.

Fh   *Vh*

Left hand, palm up and right, fingers away and right; right hand palm down, fingers away and left. Fingers of right hand on palm of left.

Oh   *Fh*

Left palm right and toward, fingers away and right; right palm up, fingers away and left. Left hand on centre of right palm.

13. SELF-HELP SKILLS

This section covers Eating, Washing, Dressing, Toileting, Social Responsibility and Sleep. It consists of interview items which can in general be completed with the cooperation of the teacher, nurse or parent or by the examiner when he knows the child thoroughly. The schedule on sleep needs to be completed with the cooperation of a parent or nurse.

Eating

SH1   What food is he able to eat?
Probes:

    (a) Does he chew and eat *solid* food with *no* problems, for example: Meat; cheese; vegetables; bread; biscuits; etc.

    (b) Does he chew and eat solid foods with *some difficulty* but manages to swallow them?

    (c) If he is *unable* to eat solid foods, can he eat *soft*, or mashed foods *without difficulty?* For example: rice pudding; potatoes etc., mashed with gravy, minced meat etc.

    (d) Does he eat soft, mashed foods with *some difficulty* and manage to swallow them?

    (e) Is he *unable* to eat *soft* or mashed foods, but able to eat finely *pulped* foods containing only tiny solids, for example: pureed foods; tinned baby foods; soft ice cream etc.?

    (f) Can he eat finely *pulped* foods containing only tiny solids with *some difficulty* and manage to swallow them?

    (g) Is he *unable* to eat finely *pulped* foods even if they only contain tiny solids?

    (h) He can *only* take liquids.

SH2   (a) Does he feed himself using a knife and fork from a plate?
      (b) Does he feed himself using a spoon from a plate or bowl?

(c) If one of the above: Does he need much encouragement to do this?
Does he make a lot of mess while eating?
(d) Does he finger feed with solid foods?
(e) Does he always have to be fed but opens his mouth to take food?
(f) Does he always have to be fed, but once the food is in his mouth manage to eat it without much difficulty?
(g) Does he always have to be fed, and does not open his mouth to take food very often?
(h) Does he always have to be fed, and once the food is in his mouth he finds difficulty in eating it?

SH3   Does he tend to eat quickly or very slowly?

SH4   Is feeding a job which causes you a lot of worry and difficulty?

SH5   Does he ever bring up any of his food after he has eaten?
(If yes, identify how often, whether a particular problem etc.)

Washing
SH6   Does he wash his hands and face by himself?
Can you describe what happens?
Probes:

1. Does not wash himself - he passively accepts being washed.
2. Does not wash himself - he struggles to avoid being washed.
3. Does not wash himself - he moans, cries, screams, shouts angrily.
4. Does not wash himself - he attempts to leave the bathroom.
5. Does not wash himself - he splashes water, overfills the basin etc.
6. Does not wash himself - he drinks or plays with the water to the exclusion of washing.
7. Does not wash himself - he undresses and throws his clothes about.

8. Does not wash himself - he places clothes or other objects in water.

9. Does not wash himself (describe other problem behaviours reported).

10. Does not like being washed - objects.

SH7   Can he do any of the following things?
       (Probe to see if he does them readily or with encouragement.)

    (a) Takes himself to the bathroom.
    (b) Runs the water without problem.
    (c) Washes himself.
    (d) Empties sink without problem.
    (e) Leaves the bathroom clean and tidy.

SH8   If he tries to wash but has difficulties, are any of the following problems the cause?

1. He is profoundly handicapped and does not participate actively.

2. He has a physical handicap which makes help necessary.

3. He washes hands acceptably when supervised and encouraged - without any other assistance.

4. As yet he has not learned all the skills involved and needs some help.

5. Although he has the necessary skills to wash himself, he is likely to make too much mess and so has to be washed or supervised.

SH9   Which are the problems that cause difficulty?
       Probes:

1. Lacks skill or needs help in: filling and emptying the basin, putting in plug, removing plug, turning on tap, rinsing basin, getting water temperature correct.

2. Lacks skill or needs help in using the soap.

3. Lacks skill or needs help in using the flannel.

4. Lacks skill or needs help in judging when washing has been completed acceptably.

5. Lacks skill or needs help in using the towel to dry himself acceptably.

Bathing

SH10 Does he like bath time?
Probes:

(a) Usually takes himself to the bathroom.
(b) Usually runs own bath without problems.
(c) Usually undresses himself.
(d) Usually gets into the water by himself.
(e) Usually washes himself.
(f) Usually dries himself acceptably.
(g) Usually empties bath without problems.
(h) Usually leaves bathroom clean and tidy.

SH11 Which are the problems that cause difficulty?
Probes:

1. Lacks skill or needs help in filling and emptying the bath.
2. Lacks skill or needs help in using the soap.
3. Lacks skill or needs help in using the flannel.
4. Lacks skill or needs help in judging when bathing has been completed satisfactorily.
5. Lacks skill or needs help in using the towel to dry himself acceptably.
6. Lacks skill or needs help in dressing after bathing.

SH12 If he does not like being bathed what does he do?
Probes:

Passive acceptance
Struggles

Cries, screams
Tries to leave
Splashes water
Throws clothes in bath
Other problems

SH13   What do you do about hairwashing?
   Probes:
   Passive acceptance
   Struggles
   Cries, screams
   Tries to leave
   Splashes water
   Throws clothes in bath
   Other problems
   (If other problems) How much of a problem are these ways of going
   on? For instance does it need two of you to wash his hair?

Dressing
SH14   Does he dress himself or do you have to dress him?
   Probes:
   Puts on all clothes or just a few.
   Can he handle zips and buttons?
   Will he dress when you tell him to or do you have to encourage
   him or keep on at him all the time?

SH15   How about undressing? Does he undress himself or do you have
   to help a lot?
   Probes:
   Undoing buttons etc.

SH16   Does he ever put on other people's clothes?
   Probe:
   Is this accident or fun?

SH17   Does he ever take his clothes off when he shouldn't do so?
   Probe:
   Why do you think he does it?

Toileting (Night)

SH18 Does he remain dry all night without potting?

SH19 If potted does he remain dry at night?

(Day)

SH20 Does he manage all his own toileting needs during the day without accident?
    If he needs help with toileting does he ask you in time when help is needed?

(Accidents)

SH21 If an 'accident' does happen does he always show you he needs changing?
    If he is potted regularly does he stay dry?
    If he is potted regularly does he stay clean?
    How frequently do you put him on the pot?

>   After all set meals
>   Twice a day
>   Once a day
>   Other schedule — describe

SH22 When he takes himself to the toilet what happens? Probe as necessary and get estimate of reliability. Can he:
    Find the toilet (How about strange places?)
    Open door
    Get onto toilet seat
    Get off toilet seat
    Flush pan
    Wash hands
    Dry hands
    Pull trousers down
    Pull pants down
    Lift dress
    Pull trousers up
    Pull pants up
    Rearrange dress

Undo buttons involved
Undo zip involved
Do up buttons involved
Do up zip involved
Tries to wipe self clean
Effectively wipes self clean

SH23   Are there any problems in toileting not yet covered?
       Probes:
                   Gets up from pot or toilet before finishing
                   Wets outside pot or toilet
                   Defecates outside pot or toilet
                   Throws or smears faeces
                   Plays with faeces

Social Responsibility
SH24   Will he do simple household jobs such as:
       Sweeping the floor;
       Laying the table;
       Bringing in the milk etc.?
       Can you describe the kind of thing he does?
       Does he usually start doing the jobs you have mentioned on his
       own initiative; after it has been demonstrated; when told to do it;
       when made to do it.
       Can he be left alone to complete a job?

SH25   Does the child understand danger? Does he prevent accidents or
       avoid them?
       e.g. Pushes crockery on edge of table to middle to prevent it falling;
       Is wary when walking near children riding on swings or playing
       rough games.
       Please give examples.
       How is he on the roads or when you are out in shops? Does he run
       away?

       If an accident happens will he tell you, or show you in some way
       e.g. Does he point out a spilt drink to you; take you to a child who is
       hurt.
       Please give examples.

SH26 How does he look after his clothes?
Probes:
Is upset if he tears or rips his clothes accidently.
Folds and tidies clothes away on undressing.
Piles clothes together, without folding on undressing.
Throws clothes aside when undressing.
Takes clothes off during day and loses them.
Tears and pulls his clothes apart.
Any other troublesome behaviour.
Does he know that certain clothes are his own? e.g. will he pick them out from amongst other toys?
Please give examples.

SH27 Does he look after his own toys? e.g. Gathers them up; keeps them in a box or locker etc.
Please give examples.

Is he likely to damage other children's toys?
Does he take other children's toys?

SH28 If he breaks a toy how does this usually happen?
Probes:
Toys are *usually* broken *accidentally* — the toys being used correctly.
Toys are *usually* broken as a result of being used *incorrectly*.
Toys are *usually* broken *deliberately*.
Does he ever spoil or destroy things at home either by accident or on purpose?
Probes:
Furniture being broken, jumping, climbing, pushing over, tearing curtains etc. Marking walls, scratching tables, breaking crockery etc.

Sleep
SH29 How about sleeping? What time does he go to bed at night?
Does he usually go to bed easily?
Does he usually stay in bed once he is there?
Does he fall asleep straight away?

What does he do if he lies awake?
Is this a problem?
Does he have his own room?

SH30   Does he sleep all night?
How often does he wake at night?
Probes:
Cause
What parents do.
Whether problem to parents.

SH31   What time does he wake?
What does he do when he wakes?
Are there any problems in the morning?

SH32   Does he sleep at all during the day?
Probe:
When, how long, regularity, cause.

SH33   Do you give him anything to help him sleep?

Score Sheets
and Lattices

Section 1: Reinforcement and experience

R1, 2, 3. Effective Rewards

1. .... 2. ....

3. .... 4. ....

5. ....

R4 to 13. Preferred Activities

1. ....

2. ....

3. ....

4. ....

5. ....

R14, 15. Best Toys and Games

1. .... 2. ....

3. .... 4. ....

5. ....

Section 2: Inspection: I

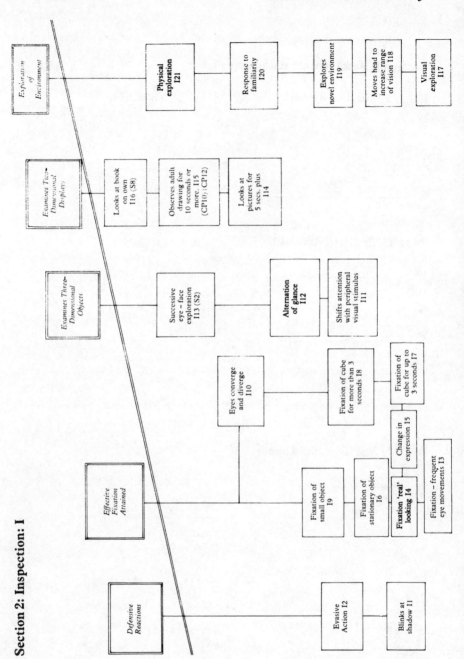

Section 3: Tracking: T

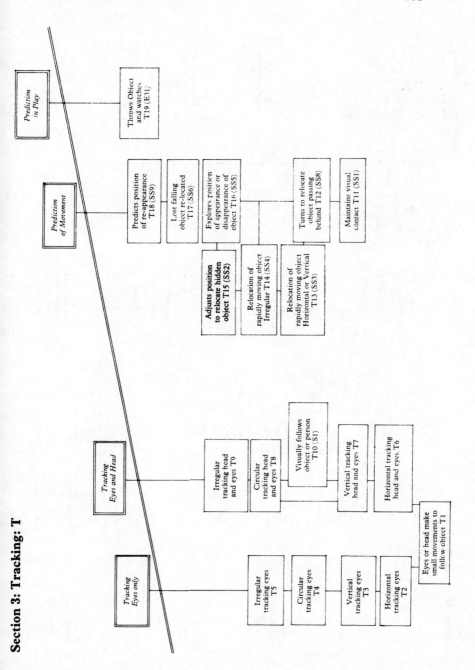

Prediction in Play

Throws Object and watches T19 (E31)

Prediction of Movement

Predicts position of re-appearance T18 (SS9)

Lost falling object re-located T17 (SS6)

Explores position of appearance or disappearance of object T16 (SS5)

Adjusts position to relocate hidden object T15 (SS2)

Relocation of rapidly moving object Irregular T14 (SS4)

Relocation of rapidly moving object Horizontal or Vertical T13 (SS3)

Turns to relocate object passing behind T12 (SS8)

Maintains visual contact T11 (SS1)

Tracking Eyes and Head

Irregular tracking head and eyes T9

Circular tracking head and eyes T8

Visually follows object or person T10 (S1)

Vertical tracking head and eyes T7

Horizontal tracking head and eyes, T6

Eyes or head make small movements to follow object T1

Tracking Eyes only

Irregular tracking eyes T5

Circular tracking eyes T4

Vertical tracking eyes T3

Horizontal tracking eyes T2

Section 4: Visuo-motor: V

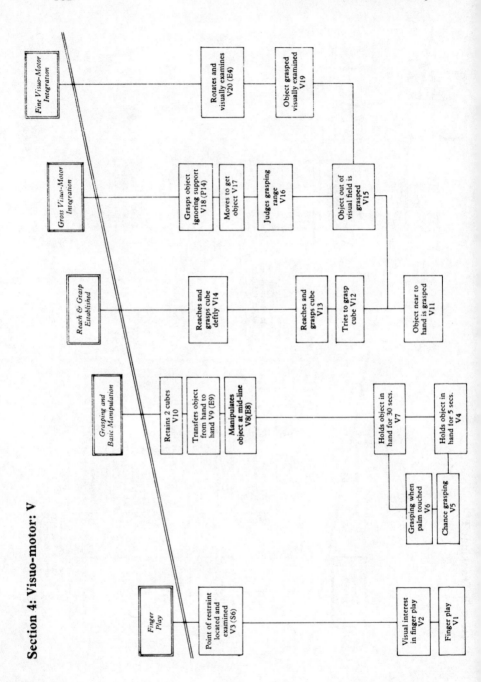

Finger Play	Grasping and Basic Manipulation	Reach & Grasp Established	Gross Visuo-Motor Integration	Fine Visuo-Motor Integration
Point of restraint located and examined V3 (S6)	Retains 2 cubes V10	Reaches and grasps cube deftly V14	Grasps object ignoring support V18 (P14)	Rotates and visually examines V20 (E4)
	Transfers object from hand to hand V9 (E9)		Moves to get object V17	Object grasped visually examined V19
	Manipulates object at mid-line V8(E8)		Judges grasping range V16	
	Holds object in hand for 30 secs. V7	Reaches and grasps cube V13	Object out of visual field is grasped V15	
	Grasping when palm touched V6	Tries to grasp cube V12		
Visual interest in finger play V2	Holds object in hand for 5 secs. V4	Object near to hand is grasped V11		
Finger play V1	Chance grasping V5			

Section 5: Auditory: A, AR

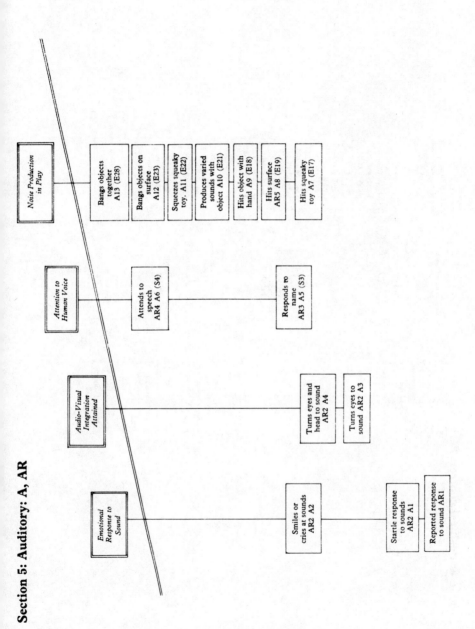

Noise Production in Play

- Bangs objects together A13 (E28)
- Bangs objects on surface A12 (E23)
- Squeezes squeaky toy. A11 (E22)
- Produces varied sounds with object A10 (E21)
- Hits object with hand A9 (E18)
- Hits surface AR5 A8 (E19)
- Hits squeaky toy A7 (E17)

Attention to Human Voice

- Attends to speech AR4 A6 (S4)
- Responds to name AR3 A5 (S3)

Audio-Visual Integration Attained

- Turns eyes and head to sound AR2 A4
- Turns eyes to sound AR2 A3

Emotional Response to Sound

- Smiles or cries at sounds AR2 A2
- Startle response to sounds AR2 A1
- Reported response to sound AR1

Section 6: Postural control: PC

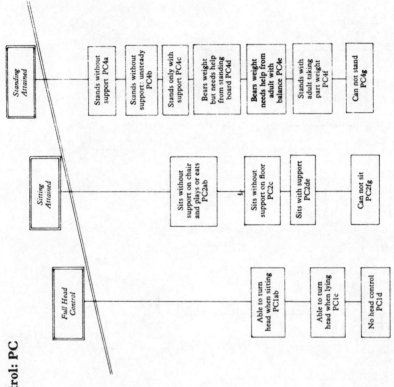

Standing Attained	Sitting Attained	Full Head Control
Stands without support PC4a	Sits without support on chair and plays or eats PC2ab	Able to turn head when sitting PC1ab
Stands without support: unsteady PC4b	Sits without support on floor PC2c	Able to turn head when lying PC1c
Stands only with support PC4c	Sits with support PC2de	No head control PC1d
Bears weight but needs help from standing board PC4d	Can not sit PC2fg	
Bears weight needs help from adult with balance PC4e		
Stands with adult taking part weight PC4f		
Can not stand PC4g		

Section 7: Exploratory play: E

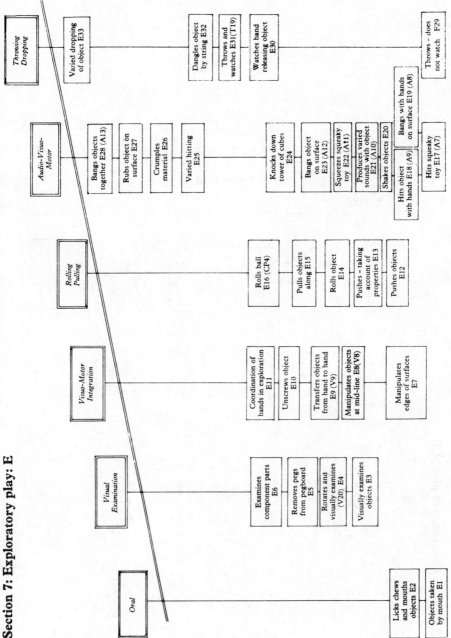

Oral
- Licks chews and mouths objects E2
- Objects taken by mouth E1

Visual Examination
- Examines component parts E6
- Removes pegs from pegboard E5
- Rotates and visually examines (V20) E4
- Visually examines objects E3

Visuo-Motor Integration
- Coordination of hands in exploration E11
- Unscrews object E10
- Transfers objects from hand to hand E9 (V9)
- Manipulates objects at mid-line E8(V8)
- Manipulates edges of surfaces E7

Rolling Pulling
- Rolls ball E16 (CP4)
- Pulls objects along E15
- Rolls object E14
- Pushes – taking account of properties E13
- Pushes objects E12

Audio-Visuo-Motor
- Bangs objects together E28 (A13)
- Rubs object on surface E27
- Crumples material E26
- Varied hitting E25
- Knocks down tower of cubes E24
- Bangs object on surface E23 (A12)
- Squeezes squeaky toy E22 (A11)
- Produces varied sounds with object E21 (A10)
- Shakes objects E20
- Hits object with hands E18 (A9)
- Bangs with hands on surface E19 (A8)
- Hits squeaky toy E17 (A7)

Throwing Dropping
- Varied dropping of object E33
- Dangles object by string E32
- Throws and watches E31(T19)
- Watches hand releasing object E30
- Throws – does not watch F29

Section 8: Constructive play: CP

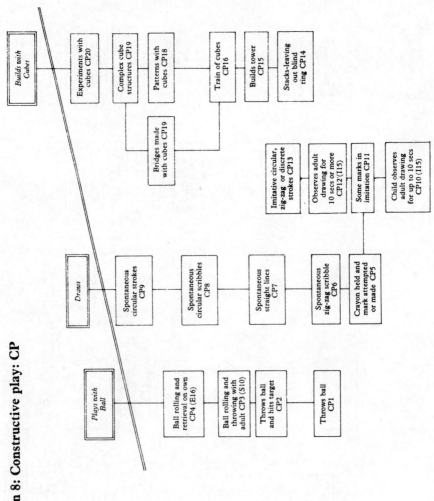

Plays with Ball

Ball rolling and retrieval on own CP4 (E16)

Ball rolling and throwing with adult CP3 (S10)

Throws ball and hits target CP2

Throws ball CP1

Draws

Spontaneous circular strokes CP9

Spontaneous circular scribbles CP8

Spontaneous straight lines CP7

Spontaneous zig-zag scribble CP6

Crayon held and mark attempted or made CP5

Imitative circular, zig-zag or discrete strokes CP13

Observes adult drawing for 10 secs or more CP12 (I15)

Some marks in imitation CP11

Child observes adult drawing for up to 10 secs CP10 (I15)

Builds with Cubes

Experiments with cubes CP20

Complex cube structures CP19

Bridges made with cubes CP19

Patterns with cubes CP18

Train of cubes CP16

Builds tower CP15

Stacks-leaving out blind ring CP14

Section 9: Search strategies: SS

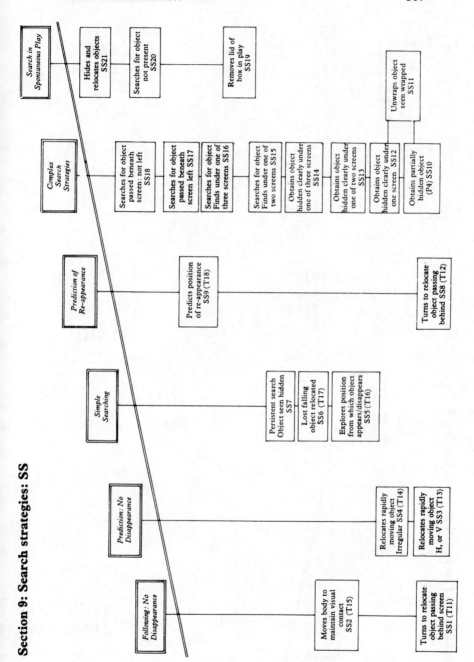

Search in Spontaneous Play
- Hides and relocates objects SS21
- Searches for object not present SS20
- Removes lid of box in play SS19

Complex Search Strategies
- Searches for object passed beneath screen: not left SS18
- Searches for object passed beneath screen left SS17
- Searches for object Finds under one of three screens SS16
- Searches for object Finds under one of two screens SS15
- Obtains object hidden clearly under one of three screens SS14
- Obtains object hidden clearly under one of two screens SS13
- Obtains object hidden clearly under one screen SS12
- Obtains partially hidden object (P4) SS10
- Unwraps object seen wrapped SS11

Prediction of Re-appearance
- Predicts position of re-appearance SS9 (T18)
- Turns to relocate object passing behind SS8 (T12)

Simple Searching
- Persistent search Object seen hidden SS7
- Lost falling object relocated SS6 (T17)
- Explores position from which object appears/disappears SS5 (T16)

Prediction: No Disappearance
- Relocates rapidly moving object Irregular SS4 (T14)
- Relocates rapidly moving object H, or V SS3 (T13)

Following: No Disappearance
- Moves body to maintain visual contact SS2 (T15)
- Turns to relocate object passing behind screen SS1 (T11)

Section 10: Perceptual problem solving: P

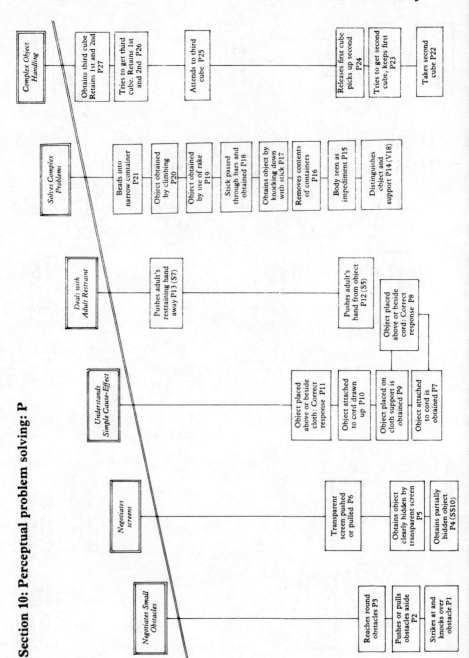

Negotiates Small Obstacles
- Reaches round obstacles P3
- Pushes or pulls obstacles aside P2
- Strikes at and knocks over obstacle P1

Negotiates screens
- Transparent screen pushed or pulled P6
- Obtains object clearly hidden by transparent screen P5
- Obtains partially hidden object P4 (SS10)

Understands Simple Cause-Effect
- Object placed above or beside cloth: Correct response P11
- Object attached to cord drawn up P10
- Object placed on cloth support is obtained P9
- Object attached to cord is obtained P7

Deals with Adult Restraint
- Pushes adult's restraining hand away P13 (S7)
- Pushes adult's hand from object P12 (S5)
- Object placed above or beside cord: Correct response P8

Solves Complex Problems
- Beads into narrow container P21
- Object obtained by climbing P20
- Object obtained by use of rake P19
- Stick passed through bars and obtained P18
- Obtains object by knocking down with stick P17
- Removes contents of containers P16
- Body seen as impediment P15
- Distinguishes object and support P14 (V18)

Complex Object Handling
- Obtains third cube Retains 1st and 2nd P27
- Tries to get third cube. Retains 1st and 2nd P26
- Attends to third cube P25
- Releases first cube picks up second P24
- Tries to get second cube, keeps first P23
- Takes second cube P22

Section 11: Social: So

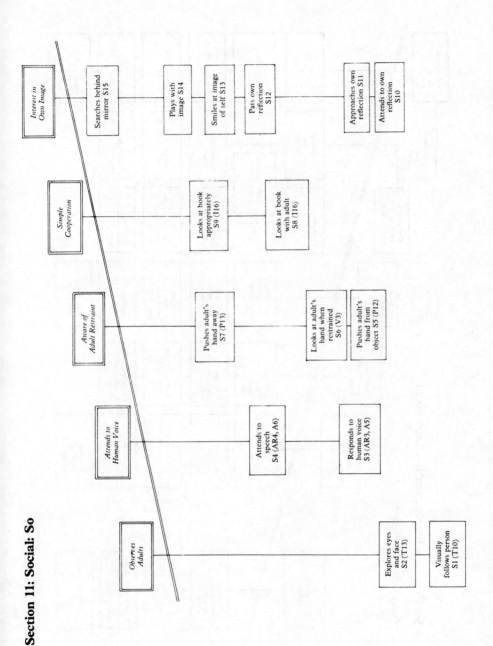

Observes Adults
- Explores eyes and face S2 (T13)
- Visually follows person S1 (T10)

Attends to Human Voice
- Attends to speech S4 (AR4, A6)
- Responds to human voice S3 (AR3, A5)

Aware of Adult Restraint
- Pushes adult's hand away S7 (P13)
- Looks at adult's hand when restrained S6 (V3)
- Pushes adult's hand from object S5 (P12)

Simple Cooperation
- Looks at book appropriately S9 (I16)
- Looks at book with adult S8 (I16)

Interest in Own Image
- Searches behind mirror S15
- Plays with image S14
- Smiles at image of self S13
- Pats own reflection S12
- Approaches own reflection S11
- Attends to own reflection S10

Section 12: Communication Interview:
Receptive Abilities

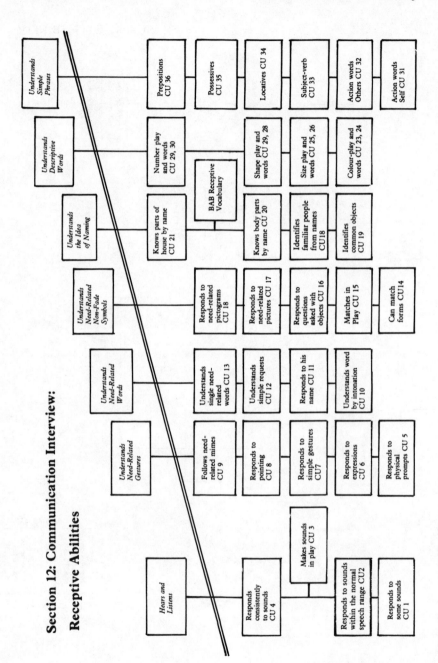

Section 12: Communication Interview: Sounds and Imitation

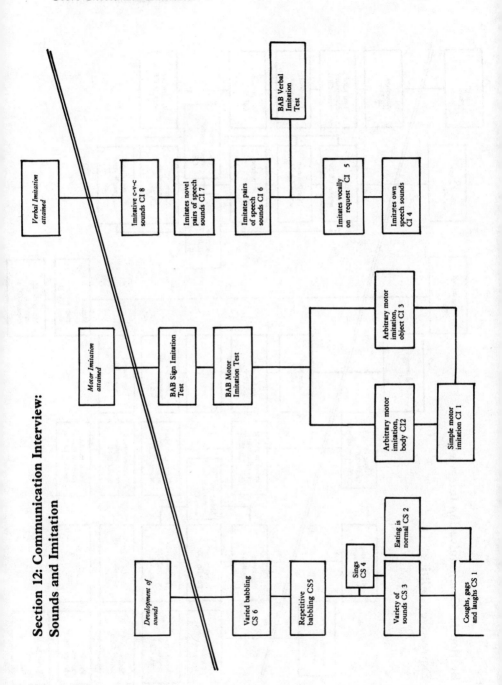

Verbal Imitation attained
- Imitative c-v-c sounds CI 8
- Imitates novel pairs of speech sounds CI 7
- Imitates pairs of speech sounds CI 6
    - BAB Verbal Imitation Test
- Imitates vocally on request CI 5
- Imitates own speech sounds CI 4

Motor Imitation attained
- BAB Sign Imitation Test
- BAB Motor Imitation Test
    - Arbitrary motor imitation, object CI 3
    - Arbitrary motor imitation, body CI 2
    - Simple motor imitation CI 1

Development of sounds
- Varied babbling CS 6
- Repetitive babbling CS 5
- Sings CS 4
- Eating is normal CS 2
- Variety of sounds CS 3
- Coughs, gags and laughs CS 1

Section 12: Communication Interview:

Expressive Abilities

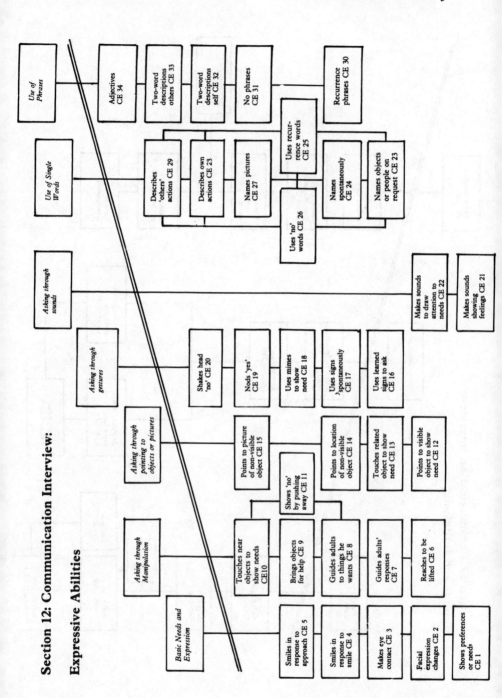

Section 13: Self-help skills: SH

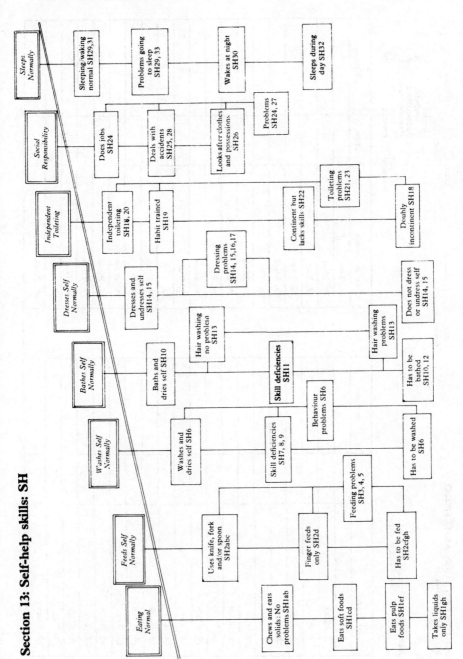

MOTOR IMITATION ASSESSMENT
PRE-TRAINING

Name ....   Date ....   Time ....
Location ....   Tester ....

Behaviours   Squeaky toy
                  Drop block in cup.

Correct   C
No Response   N
Approximate   A
Inappropriate I
Verbal   Prompt   VP
Physical   Prompt   PP

Trial Behaviour	Attn.	Response	Trial Behaviour	Attn.	Response
1. Toy			21. Toy		
2. Block			22. Block		
3. Block			23. Toy		
4. Toy			24. Toy		
5. Block			25. Block		
6. Toy			26. Toy		
7. Toy			27. Block		
8. Block			28. Block		
9. Toy			29. Toy		
10. Block			30. Block		
11. Toy			31. Toy		
12. Toy			32. Toy		
13. Block			33. Block		
14. Block			34. Toy		
15. Toy			35. Block		
16. Block			36. Block		
17. Toy			37. Toy		
18. Block			38. Toy		
19. Toy			39. Block		
20. Block			40. Block		

MOTOR IMITATION ASSESSMENT

Name .... Date .... Time ....

Location .... Tester ....

Correct – C   No Response – N   Approximate – A   Inappropriate – I

LIST 1 Behaviours – see definitions

LIST 1

Trial Behaviour	Attn.	Resp.	Trial Behaviour	Attn.	Resp.
1. Ring bells			16. Cup in cup		
2. Push car			17. Put on hat		
3. Stir with spoon			18. Roll ball		
4. Put on hat			19. Beat drum		
5. Roll ball			20. Pull lorry		
6. Beat drum			21. Bracelet		
7. Stack barrels			22. Stir with spoon		
8. Pull lorry			23. Stir with spoon		
9. Cup in cup			24. Cup in cup		
10. Bracelet			25. Roll ball		
11. Stir with spoon			26. Beat drum		
12. Push car			27. Pull lorry		
13. Ring bells			28. Stack barrels		
14. Stack barrels			29. Push car		
15. Bracelet			30. Put on hat		

LIST 2

Trial Behaviour	Attn.	Resp.	Trial Behaviour	Attn.	Resp.
1. Comb			16. Pick up object		
2. Rub hands			17. Finger on nose		
3. Draw			18. Block in box		
4. Block in box			19. Hands on head		
5. Slap thighs			20. Rub hands		
6. Raise arm			21. Blow whistle		
7. Blow whistle			22. Pick up object		
8. Finger on nose			23. Raise arm		
9. Pick up object			24. Hands on head		
10. Hands on head			25. Rub hands		
11. Comb			26. Draw		
12. Draw			27. Block in box		
13. Blow whistle			28. Comb		
14. Slap thighs			29. Slap thighs		
15. Raise arm			30. Finger on nose		

Score: **LIST 1** Correct .... No Response .... Approximate .... Inappropriate ....

       LIST 2 Correct .... No Response .... Approximate .... Inappropriate ....

VERBAL IMITATION ASSESSMENT
PRE-TRAINING

Stimulus sounds: a – as in father   mm – long m

Attn. Record (v) if child was attending.

Name................................   Date................   Time................
Location................................   Tester................

Correct   C
No Response   N
Unintelligible   U
Other(Transcribe)   T

Trial	Sound	Attn.	Resp.	Trial	Sound	Attn.	Resp.
1	a			21	a		
2	mmm			22	a		
3	mmm			23	mmm		
4	a			24	a		
5	a			25	mmm		
6	mmm			26	a		
7	a			27	mmm		
8	mmm			28	mmm		
9	a			29	a		
10	a			30	mmm		
11	mmm			31	a		
12	mmm			32	a		
13	a			33	mmm		
14	mmm			34	mmm		
15	a			35	a		
16	mmm			36	mmm		
17	a			37	mmm		
18	a			38	a		
19	mmm			39	mmm		
20	mmm			40	a		

Comment

VERBAL IMITATION ASSESSMENT
(TAPE RECORD)

Name .... Location .... Date .... Tester .... Time ....

Correct – C   or   No Response – N   or   Unintelligible – UT   or   Other (transcribe)

LIST 1

1.	b as in boy	9.	k as in cat	17.	t as in toy
2.	m as in man	10.	h as in hat	18.	b as in boy
3.	d as in dog	11.	t as in toy	19.	n as in no
4.	n as in no	12.	w as in way	20.	s as in see
5.	p as in pipe	13.	m as in man	21.	k as in cat
6.	s as in see	14.	p as in pipe	22.	w as in way
7.	f as in fat	15.	g as in go	23.	h as in hat
8.	g as in go	16.	f as in fat	24.	d as in dog

If child gets first twelve correct – terminate and go to List 2. If child gets 8 out of 24 go to List 2. Less than eight administer List 2 if in doubt about failure.

Comments

LIST 2

1.	bang	9.	saw	17.	no
2.	car	10.	teeth	18.	bang
3.	dog	11.	watch	19.	teeth
4.	good	12.	mother	20.	mother
5.	hoop	13.	good	21.	pie
6.	mouse	14.	car	22.	dog
7.	no	15.	mouse	23.	hoop
8.	pie	16.	watch	24.	saw

If child imitates well on first 12 terminate and go to List 3. If child gets eight out of 24 go to List 3. Less than eight go on if in doubt about failure.

Comments

RECEPTIVE VOCABULARY ASSESSMENT
PRE-TRAINING
Stimulus Items: Hat : Baby

Name................ Date................ Time................
Location................ Tester................

Trial	Object	Appropriate	Inappropriate	Trial	Object	Appropriate	Inappropriate
1.	Hat			21.	Hat		
2.	Baby			22.	Hat		
3.	Hat			23.	Baby		
4.	Hat			24.	Baby		
5.	Baby			25.	Hat		
6.	Hat			26.	Baby		
7.	Baby			27.	Hat		
8.	Baby			28.	Hat		
9.	Hat			29.	Baby		
10.	Hat			30.	Baby		
11.	Baby			31.	Hat		
12.	Hat			32.	Hat		
13.	Baby			33.	Baby		
14.	Baby			34.	Baby		
15.	Hat			35.	Hat		
16.	Baby			36.	Hat		
17.	Hat			37.	Baby		
18.	Baby			38.	Baby		
19.	Hat			39.	Hat		
20.	Baby			40.	Baby		

RECEPTIVE VOCABULARY ASSESSMENT

Name............................... Date............. Time.............
Location.................... Tester.............

Correct C   or   No Response NR   or   Incorrect I   or   Other (Transcribe)

LIST 1.

Attn: Record (√) if child was attending   Object to be presented is indicated in heavy type.

Stimulus	Attn.	Resp.	Stimulus	Attn.	Resp.	Stimulus	Attn.	Resp.
1.			11.			21.		
2.			12.			22.		
3.			13.			23.		
4.			14.			24.		
5.			15.			25.		
6.			16.			26.		
7.			17.			27.		
8.			18.			28.		
9.			19.			29.		
10.			20.			30.		

LIST 2.

Stimulus	Object	Stimulus	Object	Stimulus	Object
1.		11.		21.	
2.		12.		22.	
3.		13.		23.	
4.		14.		24.	
5.		15.		25.	
6.		16.		26.	
7.		17.		27.	
8.		18.		28.	
9.		19.		29.	
10.		20.		30.	

Tested in Speech: Sign: Symbols: lip reading: sound only. Tested with objects: colour pictures: line drawings.

EXPRESSIVE VOCABULARY ASSESSMENT
PRE-TRAINING

Stimulus Objects: Bottle : Flower

Name .... Date .... Time ....
Location .... Tester ....

Correct	C
No Response	N
Approximate	A
Inappropriate	I
Verbal Prompt	VP
Physical Prompt	PP

Attn: Record (√) if child was attending

Trial	Object	Attn.	Resp.	Trial	Object	Attn.	Resp.	Trial	Object	Attn.	Resp.	Trial	Object	Attn.	Resp.
1.	Bottle			11.	Bottle			21.	Bottle			31.	Bottle		
2.	Flower			12.	Flower			22.	Flower			32.	Flower		
3.	Flower			13.	Bottle			23.	Bottle			33.	Flower		
4.	Bottle			14.	Flower			24.	Flower			34.	Bottle		
5.	Flower			15.	Bottle			25.	Bottle			35.	Bottle		
6.	Flower			16.	Bottle			26.	Flower			36.	Flower		
7.	Bottle			17.	Flower			27.	Flower			37.	Bottle		
8.	Flower			18.	Flower			28.	Bottle			38.	Flower		
9.	Flower			19.	Bottle			29.	Flower			39.	Flower		
10.	Bottle			20.	Flower			30.	Bottle			40.	Bottle		

Tested in Speech: Sign: Symbols. Tested with Objects: Colour pictures: Line drawings.

EXPRESSIVE VOCABULARY ASSESSMENT

Name.. Date................................ Time................................

Location.. Tester................................

Correct – C   Incorrect – I   No Response – N   Disruptive – D

A - Approximate

LIST 1

1.					
2.					
3.					
4.					
5.					
6.					
7.					
8.					
9.					
10.					
11.					
12.					
13.					
14.					
15.					

LIST 2

1.					
2.					
3.					
4.					
5.					
6.					
7.					
8.					
9.					
10.					
11.					
12.					
13.					
14.					
15.					

Score: LIST 1. Correct................ No Response................ Incorrect................ Disruptive................ Approximate................

LIST 2. Correct................ No Response................ Incorrect................ Disruptive................ Approximate................

Tested in Speech: Sign: Symbols. Tested with Objects: Colour pictures: Line drawings: Lip-reading: Objects (sign): Objects (symbol).

REFERENCES

ALPERT, C. (1980). 'Procedures for determining the optimal non-speech mode for the autistic child'. In: SCHIEFELBUSCH, R. L. (Ed) *Nonspeech Language and Communication: Analysis and Intervention*. Baltimore: University Park Press. pp 389-420.

AZRIN, N. and FOXX, R. (1974). *Toilet Training in Less Then a Day*. London: Macmillan.

BARON, N. S. and ISENSEE, L. M. (1976). Effectiveness of manual versus spoken language with an autistic child. Unpublished paper, Brown University, Providence, Rhode Island.

BAYLEY, N. (1969). *Bayley Scales of Infant Development*. New York: Psychological Corporation.

BENDER, M. and VALLETUTTI, J. P. (1976). *Teaching the Moderately and Severely Handicapped: Volume 1: Behaviour, Self-care and Motor Skills*. Baltimore: University Park Press.

BENDER, M., VALLETUTTI, J. P. and BENDER, R. (1976). *Teaching the Moderately and Severely Handicapped. Volume II. Communication, Socialisation, Safety and Leisure-time skills*. Baltimore: University Park Press.

BERGÉS, J. and LÈZIRE, I. (1965). *The Imitation of Gestures*. London: Spastics Society.

BERSOFF, D.N. and GREIGER, R.M. (1971). 'An interview model for the psycho-situational assessment of children's behaviour', *American Journal of Orthopsychiatry*, 1971, **41**, 483-93.

BLISS, C. (1965). *Semantography*. Sydney, Australia: Semantography publications.

BLUMA, S., SHEARER, J., FROHMAN, A. and HILLIARD, J. (1976). *Portage Guide to Early Education*. Portage, Wisconsin: Cooperative Educational Service Agency 12.

BRENNAN, M., COLVILLE, M.D. and LAWSON, L.K. (1980). *Words in Hand*. Edinburgh: Edinburgh BSL Project.

BUDDE, J. F. and MENOLASCINO, F. J. (1971). 'Systems technology and retardation: Applications to vocational habilitation', *Mental Retardation*, 1971, **9**, 11-16.

CARR, E.G. (1979). 'Teaching autistic children to use sign language: Some research issues', *Journal of Autism and Developmental Disorders*, 1979, **9**, 345-59.

CARR, E. G., BINKOFF, J. A., KOLOGINSKY, B. and EDDY, M. (1978). 'Acquisition of sign language by autistic children. 1. Expressive labelling', *Journal of Applied Behaviour Analysis*, 1978, **11**, 489-501.

CARR, E. G. and DORES, P. A. (1981). 'Patterns of language acquisition following simultaneous communication with autistic children', *Analysis and Intervention in Developmental Disabilities*, 1981, **1**, 1-15.

CARR, J. (1980). *Helping Your Handicapped Child*. Harmondsworth: Penguin.

CHURCHILL, D. W. (1978). *Language of Autistic Children*. New York: John Wiley.

CLARK, C.R. and WOODCOCK, R.W. (1976). 'Graphic systems of communication'. In: LLOYD, L. L. (Ed) *Communication, Assessment and Intervention Strategies*. Baltimore: University Park Press. pp 549-605.

CLARKE, A. D. B. and CLARKE, A. M. (1973). 'Assessment and prediction'. In: MITTLER, P. (Ed) *Assessment for Learning in the Mentally Handicapped*. London: Churchill Livingstone. pp 23-39.

CONNOR, F. P. and TALBOT, M. E. (undated). *An Experimental Curriculum for Young Mentally Retarded Children*. New York: Teachers College Press.

CRAIG, E. (1978). 'Introducing the Paget Gorman Sign System'. In: TEBBS, T. (Ed) *Ways and Means*. Basingstoke: Globe Education.

CRATTY, B. J. (1970). *Perceptual and Motor Development in Infants and Young Children*. New York: Collier Macmillan.

CREGAN, A. (1982). 'The development and use of Sigsymbols'. In: KIERNAN, C. C. (Ed) *Routes to Communication: Studies in the Use of Non-Vocal Communication Systems with the Handicapped*. Tunbridge Wells: Costello Educational. (In Press.)

CUNNINGHAM, C. and SLOPER, P. (1978). *Helping Your Handicapped Baby*. London: Souvenir Press.

CURCIO, F. (1978). 'Sensorimotor functioning and communication in mute autistic children', *Journal of Autism and Childhood Schizophrenia*, 1978, **8**, 281-92.

DOLL, E. A. (1953). *The Measurement of Social Competence*. Minneapolis: Educational Test Bureau.

DUNST, C. J. (1980). *A Clinical and Educational Manual for Use with the Uzgiris and Hunt Scales of Infant Psychological Development*. Baltimore: University Park Press.

EDWARDS, A. L. (1957). *Techniques of Attitude Scale Construction*. New York: Appleton Century Crofts.

FINNIE, N. R. (1974). *Handling the Young Cerebral Palsied Child at Home*. Second Edition. London: William Heinemann.

FOXEN, T. and MCBRIEN, J. (1981). *Training Staff in Behavioural Methods: The EDY In-Service Course for Mental Handicap Practitioners*. Manchester: Manchester University Press.

FRISTOE, M. and LLOYD, L. L. (1979). 'Non-speech communication'. In: ELLIS, N. R. (Ed) *Handbook of Mental Deficiency: Psychological Theory and Research*. Second Edition. New York: Laurence Erlbaum.

FROSTIG, M., LEFEVER, D. W. and WHITTLESEY, J. R. B. (1964). *The Marianne Frostig Developmental Test of Visual Perception*. Palo Alto, California: Consulting Psychologists Press.

GLASER, R. (1963). 'Instructional technology and the measurement of learning outcomes: some questions', *American Psychologist*, 1963, **18**, 519-21.

GOODENOUGH, W. H. (1944). 'A technique for scale analysis', *Educational and Psychological Measurement*, 1944, **4**, 179-90.

GOODFRIEND, R. S. (1972). *Power in Perception for the Young Child*. New York: Teachers College Press.

GREEN, B. F. (1956). 'A method of scalogram analysis using summary statistics', *Psychometrika*, 1956, **21**, 79-88.

GUNZBURG, H. C. (1973). *Progress Assessment Charts*. London: NAMH.

HOLLINSHEAD, W. H. (1960). *Functional Anatomy of the Limbs and Back*. Edinburgh: Livingstone.

HOLLIS, J. H. and CARRIER, J. K. Jr. (1978). 'Intervention strategies for nonspeech children'. In: SCHIEFELBUSCH, R. L. (Ed) *Language Intervention Strategies*. Baltimore: University Park Press. pp 57-100.

HOUSE, B. J., HANLEY, M. J. and MAGID, D. F. (1980). 'Logographic reading by TMR adults', *American Journal of Mental Deficiency*, 1980, **85**, 161-70.

INGRAM, D. (1976). *Phonological Disability in Children*. London: Arnold.

JEDRYSEK, E., KLAPPER, Z., POPE, L. and WORTIS, J. (1972). *Psycho-educational Evaluation of the Preschool child*. New York and London: Grune Stratton.

JEFFREE, D. and MCCONKEY, R. (1976). *Let Me Speak*. London: Souvenir Press.

JEFFREE, D., MCCONKEY, R. and HEWSON, S. (1979). *Let Me Play*. London: Souvenir Press.

JONES, H. (1972). *Talking Hands*. London: Stanley Paul.

JONES, L. M., REID, B. D. and KIERNAN, C. C. (1982). 'Signs and symbols: the 1980 survey.' In: PETER, M. and BARNES, R. (Eds). *Signs, Symbols and Schools*. Stratford: National Council for Special Education. Also published in (1982) *Special Education: Forward Trends*, **9**, 2, 34-7.

JONES, M. C. (1971). A development schedule based on Piaget's sensori-motor writings: an examination of the schedule's potential value as an instrument for assessing severely and profoundly subnormal children. Unpublished masters thesis: University of London Institute of Education.

JONES, M. S. and KIERNAN, C. C. (1981). Sign 'articulation' training for a mentally handicapped girl. Unpublished manuscript. Thomas Coram Research Unit.

JUVONEN, L. A. (1972). Development of play behaviour in two severely retarded children. Unpublished Masters thesis: University of London Institute of Education.

KIERNAN, C. C. (1973). 'Functional analysis'. In: MITTLER, P. (Ed) *Assessment for Learning in the Mentally Handicapped*. London: Churchill Livingstone.

KIERNAN, C. C. (1974). 'Behaviour modification'. In: CLARKE, A. D. B. and CLARKE, A. M. (Eds). *Mental Deficiency: The Changing Outlook*. London: Methuen. pp 729-803.

KIERNAN, C. C. (1975). 'Experimental investigation of the curriculum for the profoundly handicapped.' In: TIZARD, J. (Ed) *Mental Retardation: Concepts of Education and Research*. London: Butterworths. pp 57-79.

KIERNAN, C. C. (1977). 'Toward a curriculum for the profoundly retarded multiply handicapped child', *Child: Care Health and Development*, 1977, **3**, 229-39.

KIERNAN, C. C. (1978). Summary of work from 1975-1978. Report to the Department of Health and Social Security.

KIERNAN, C. C. (1980). 'General principles of curriculum planning'. In: CRAWFORD, N. (Ed). *Curriculum Planning for the ESN(S) Child*. Kidderminster: BIMH.

KIERNAN, C. C. (1981a). 'A strategy for research on the use of nonvocal systems of communication', *Journal of Autism and Developmental Disorders*.

KIERNAN, C. C. (1981b). *Analysis of Programmes for Teaching*. Basingstoke: Globe Education.

KIERNAN, C. C. (1982a). 'Noncore areas of the curriculum for the

ESN(S) child'. In: CRAWFORD, N. (Ed). *Curriculum Planning for the ESN(S) Child. Vol. 2.* Kidderminster: BIMH. (In press.)

KIERNAN, C. C. (1982b). 'The use of non-vocal communication techniques with autistic individuals', *Journal of Child Psychology and Psychiatry* (In press).

KIERNAN, C. C. (1982c). Social Services Involvement with the Handicapped. Final report to the Department of Health and Social Security.

KIERNAN, C. C. (1982d) 'Behaviour modification and the development of communication'. In: MITTLER, P. (Ed) *Frontiers of Knowledge in Mental Retardation Volume 1.* Baltimore: University Park Press.

KIERNAN, C. C. and JONES, M. C. (1980). 'The Behaviour Assessment Battery for use with the profoundly retarded'. In: HOGG, J. and MITTLER, P. (Eds) *Advances in Mental Handicap Research Volume 1.* London: John Wiley.

KIERNAN, C. C. and JONES, M. S. (1982). 'The Heuristic Programme: A combined use of signs and symbols with severely mentally handicapped children'. In: KIERNAN, C. C. (Ed) *Routes to Communication: Studies in the Use of Non-Vocal Communication Systems with the Handicapped.* Tunbridge Wells: Costello Education. (In press.)

KIERNAN, C. C., JORDAN, R. and SAUNDERS, C. (1978). *Starting Off.* London: Souvenir Press.

KIERNAN, C. C., KAVANAGH, S. and BAILEY, J. (1982). 'Jim and the Action Men'. In: KIERNAN, C. C. (Ed) *Routes to Communication: Studies in the Use of Non-Vocal Communication Systems with the Handicapped.* Tunbridge Wells: Costello Educational. (In press.)

KIERNAN, C. C. and REID, B. D. (1977). The Imitation Test. Unpublished manuscript, Thomas Coram Research Unit, University of London, Institute of Education.

KIERNAN, C. C., REID, B. D. and JONES, L. M. (1982). *Signs and Symbols: A review of literature and survey of use of nonvocal communication systems.* London: Studies in Education, No. 11. University of London, Institute of Education.

KIERNAN, C. C., WRIGHT, E. and HAWKS, G. (1975). 'The ward wide application of operant training techniques'. In: PRIMROSE, H. (Ed) *Proceedings of the Third International Congress of the IASSMD.* Poland: Polish Medical Publishers.

KIRK, S. A. and McCARTHY, J. P. (1961). *Illinois Test for*

Psycholinguistic Abilities. Illinois: University of Illinois Press.
KONSTANTAREAS, M. M., OXMAN, J. and WEBSTER, C. D. (1977).
'Simultaneous communication with nonverbal children: An
alternative to speech with autistic and other severely
dysfunctional non-verbal children', *Journal of Communication
Disorders*, 1977, **10**, 267-82.
KUNTZ, J. B., CARRIER, J. K. and HOLLIS, J. H. (1978). 'A nonvocal
system for teaching retarded children to read and write'. In:
MEYERS, C. (Ed) *Quality of Life in Severely Profoundly Retarded
People: Research Foundations for Improvements*. Washington:
American Association on Mental Deficiency. pp 145-91.
LEVITT, S.(1977). *Treatment of Cerebral Palsy and Motor Delay*.
Oxford: Blackwell Scientific Publications.
LOVAAS, O. I. and SCHREIBMAN, L. (1971). 'Stimulus over-
selectivity of autistic children in a two stimulus situation',
Behaviour Research and Therapy, 1971, **9**, 305-10.
McINTYRE, M. (1974). Unpublished masters thesis, California State
College, Northridge.
McREYNOLDS, L. V. and ENGMANN, D. L. (1975). *Distinctive
Feature Analysis of Misarticulations*. Baltimore: University Park
Press.
MILLER, J. F. and YODER, D. E. (1972). 'A syntax teaching program'.
In: McLEAN, D., YODER, D. and SCHIEFELBUSCH, R. (Eds)
Language Intervention with the Retarded. Baltimore: University
Park Press. pp. 191-211.
MISCHEL, W. (1968). *Personality and Assessment*. New York: Wiley.
MORALES, I. (1972). Application of operant techniques to some
aspects of exploratory behaviour of two severely retarded
children. Unpublished masters thesis, University of London
Institute of Education.
NEWSON, J. and NEWSON, E. (1979). *Toys and Playthings*.
Harmondsworth: Penguin.
PAGET, R., GORMAN, P. and PAGET, G. (1972). *A Systematic Sign
Language*. London: Mimeographed.
PANYAN, M., BOOZER, H. and MORRIS, N. (1970). 'Feedback to
attendants as a reinforcer for applying behaviour modification
techniques to the mentally retarded', *Journal of Applied Behaviour
Analysis*, 1970, **3**, 1-11.
PIAGET, J. (1952). *The Origins of Intelligence in Children*. New York:
International University Press.

PIAGET, J. (1954). *The Construction of Reality in Children.* New York: Basic Books.

REID, B. D. and KIERNAN, C. C. (1982). The effects of three methods of sign-word pairing on the subsequent learning of words. (In preparation).

RIEKEHOF, L. L. (1963). *Talk to the Deaf.* Springfield, Mo.: Gospel Publishing House.

ROBSON, C., JONES, A. and STOREY, M. (1980). *Language Development Through Structured Teaching: A minicourse for teachers of the mentally handicapped.* Project TASS: Huddersfield Polytechnic and the Hester Adrian Research Centre, University of Manchester.

RUTTER, M., GRAHAM, P. and YULE, W. (1970). *A Neuropsychiatric Study in Childhood.* London: Spastics Society.

SCHAEFFER, B., MUSIL, A. and KOLLINZAS, G. (1980). *Total Communication: A Signed Speech Program for Nonverbal Children.* Champaign, Illinois: Research Press.

SHAKESPEARE, R. (1970). 'Severely subnormal children'. In: MITTLER, P. (Ed) *The Psychological Assessment of Mental and Physical Handicaps.* London: Methuen. pp 519-41.

SILVERMAN, F. H. (1980). *Communication for the Speechless.* Englewood Cliffs, N.J.: Prentice-Hall.

STOKOE, W. C., CASTERLINE, D. C. and CRONEBERG, C. G. (1965). *Dictionary of American Sign Language on Linguistic Principles.* Washington D.C.: Gallaudet College.

SUTCLIFFE, T. H. (1971). *Conversation with the Deaf.* London: Royal National Institute for the Deaf.

UZGIRIS, I. C. and HUNT, J. McV. (1975). *Assessment in Infancy.* Urbana: University of Illinois Press.

WALKER, M. (1976). *The Makaton Vocabulary* (Revised edition). London: R.A.D.D.

WALKER, M. (1978). 'The Makaton Vocabulary.' In: TEBBS, T. (Ed) *Ways and Means.* Basingstoke: Globe Education. pp 174-84.

WEBSTER, C. D., MCPHERSON, H., SLOMAN, L., EVANS, M. A. and KUCHAR, E. (1973). 'Communicating with an autistic boy by gestures', *Journal of Autism and Childhood Schizophrenia,* 1973, **3**, 337-46.

WHITE, B. L. (1971). *Human Infants.* Englewood Cliffs, N. J.: Prentice-Hall.

WILBUR, R. B. (1979). *American Sign Language and Sign Systems.*

Baltimore: University Park Press.
WOODWARD, W. M. (1970). 'The assessment of cognitive processes: Piaget's approach'. In: MITTLER, P. (Ed) *The Psychological Assessment of Mental and Physical Handicaps*. London: Methuen. pp 695-718.